# Daddy Lessons

## Steacy Easton

Coach House Books, Toronto

first edition

Published with the generous assistance of the Canada Council for the Arts and the Ontario Arts Council. Coach House Books also acknowledges the support of the Government of Ontario through the Ontario Book Publishing Tax Credit.


LIBRARY AND ARCHIVES CANADA CATALOGUING IN PUBLICATION

Title: Daddy lessons / by Steacy Easton.
Names: Easton, Steacy, author.
Identifiers: Canadiana (print) 20230470882 | Canadiana (ebook) 20230470890 | ISBN 9781552454732 (softcover) | ISBN 9781770567849 (EPUB) | ISBN 9781770567856 (PDF)
Subjects: LCSH: Easton, Steacy. | LCSH: Sexual minorities—Prairie Provinces—Biography. | LCSH: Gender-nonconforming people—Prairie Provinces—Biography. | LCSH: Sexual orientation. | LCSH: Gender nonconformity. | LCSH: Gender identity. | LCSH: Sex. | LCGFT: Autobiographies.
Classification: LCC HQ73.73.C32 P73 2023 | DDC 306.76092—dc23


*Daddy Lessons* is available as an ebook: ISBN 978 1 77056 784 9 (EPUB); ISBN 978 1 77056 785 6 (PDF)


Purchase of the print version of this book entitles you to a free digital copy. To claim your ebook of this title, please email sales@chbooks.com with proof of purchase. (Coach House Books reserves the right to terminate the free digital download offer at any time.)

'There is no unthreatened, unthreatening conceptual home for the concept of gay origins. We have all the more reason, then, to keep our understanding of gay origin, of gay cultural and material reproduction, plural, multi-capillaried, argus-eyed, respectful, and endlessly cherished.'
– Eve Kosofsky Sedgwick, *Epistemology of the Closet*

'The "I" is the paradigmatic pornographer whose aesthetic I am trying to limn and justify … '
– Wayne Koestenbaum, 'The Darling's Prick'

'Well, sir, I ain't a for-real cowboy. But I am one helluva stud.'
– Joe Buck, *Midnight Cowboy*

'To attempt to occupy a place as speaking subject within the traditional gender frame is to become complicit in the discourse which one wishes to deconstruct.'
– Sandy Stone, 'The *Empire* Strikes Back: A Posttransexual Manifesto'

# Prologue

Learning how to hold a fork, how to hold a cock, how to parse a sentence. Learning how to parse a come-on, how to operate in an elder artist's front room, how to operate in a bathhouse. These are the same kinds of learning, but not the same form.

Learning how to be an adult is learning how to maintain an integrated self against the plurality of forms. The forms must maintain a certain kind of boundary. The precocious child is still a child; their desires are never adult desires. Their understandings are not adult understandings either. Wanting to be an adult, wanting to have adult pleasures as a child, comes from wanting to avoid the limits of childhood – the restrictions, the boredom, the exhaustion of being a child. Being a child features a lot of waiting and a lot of confusion. In Western (white, Canadian) culture, there is an obsession with the innocence of the child, a creation of childhood as a perfect Arcadian space that must be maintained well into adolescence. This is especially true of white children and middle-class children; we want to bask in the golden glow of a Spielbergian sunset without having to contend with the darkness that follows.

The central tragedy of childhood is never getting what you want. It is being trapped in that Arcadia. Some adults exploit this for their own entertainment, for their own capital, for their own pleasure, and for their own needs or wants.

I was born wanting and failing to fully satisfy what that wanting was. The more aberrant the wanting, the more complex the hunger, the less simple the ways or means of satisfying that hunger. If desire is an Arcadia, it must be noticed that the forest there is profoundly artificial; it looks like nature, but it is not nature. This unnatural nature is more of a question of how to be, as opposed to how to do; though, in a complicated way, learning how to do led me to places where I could learn how to be. The central crux was the difference between those two states: turning the doing into being and leaning on adults who I thought made those two states into one. And even if you were 'born that way,' the way is defined; the variation is formed and shaped by pleasures and questions about pleasure from the beginning.

Let's make this less abstract.

When I was eight, I was baptized into the Church of Jesus Christ of Latter-day Saints. I was sent away to an Anglican boarding school for Grades 7 and 8. I spent my next year as an in-patient at an adolescent psychiatric facility, and the following years in high school, frequenting Edmonton's bathhouses and adult theatres. After graduation: trysts with both a rodeo cowboy and a priest, a master's in theology, a sexual abuse trial for a man at that boarding school.

This book is about what it means to have hunger as a young person for adult pleasures. This book is about what it means for a young person to think they want to have adult pleasures, not knowing what adult pleasures are. This book is about what it means to push oneself into adult pleasure.

Pleasure here is of the body. Pleasure is of flesh. Pleasure is of sex, which is the third rail of this conversation – thinking of the Frank O'Hara poem:

but what about the soul
that grows in darkness, embossed by silvery images

What follows is all kinds of darkness: the darkness of the bedroom, of the backroom, of the confessional booth, the library carrel, the edges of temples and chapels, the city after dark, the car on the drive back to the suburbs. Embossed here, drawn over, raised over a flat surface, text upon text. And maybe, like most stories, just a little bit exaggerated …

Embossed like the hoary old Edwardian joke, repeated by Mae West, about going up to see someone's 'etchings.' The etchings are both a kind of pornography and a kind of lesson to teach. I am writing pornography here. Not only explicit references to sexuality, but a form meant to excite and entice the body. Here are things that enticed my body one week in September: the single pink carnation in a plain vase; the orange chicken at a snobbish, newish Chinese fusion joint; the memory of Serge Lutens's La Fille de Berlin; Beyoncé's 'Church Girl'; Loretta Lynn and Conway Twitty's 'As Soon as I Hang Up the Phone;' how Ryman fastened his paintings to the wall in 1976; mini-doughnuts at the Canadian National Exhibition; a plump boy's gorgeous tits, dark as liver, rising from a pelt of curly chestnut hair as he rides me; the pubic hair of French boys in 1954's *Nus masculins*; the yellow daisies in the same movie; the stern, austere density of Murane's essays; a friend's roast chicken and potatoes.

This book will be of the body, will be the piling of signs. It will be the lapidary pleasures, repeating, growing – not the thrust of cock and not the expectation of cumming, but not without the pearlescent gleam of fluids, of spit, of sweat, of semen.

This is pornography in the sense that it is explicit. It talks about mouths, assholes, cocks, cunts, hands – but it is the ritual of those body parts and how we write and consider those body parts. Nothing will be elided. Pornography is incidental, elliptical, anecdotal, a collapsing of form into an immediacy – maybe a little like memory, emerging, finishing the business at hand, retreating until it disappears. Maybe it's like conversation too – the kind of sloppy one after a nice dinner with too much wine, where you tell too much. Or the kind of quick and fast one in a diner that you don't remember, the fifteen-minute coffee date, the two-hour late-afternoon lunch … Maybe that's one of the arguments I am making: bodily appetite and desire, the interaction of bodies with other bodies, have a lovely little concordance – a concordance that cannot be fully understood. Eating with someone is sometimes like fucking them, and talking to someone is sometimes like fucking them, but not in the crude one-to-one correlation of plot. It's in the miasmic, free-floating reworking of material pleasures into something more abstract, the immutable warmth that I might have, in my more pious days, called the holy spirit.

————

Queerness is the outside looking in; it is orthogonal to good breeding, good manners, good taste. Orthogonal to good manners does not mean absent from any manners; the demi-monde has its own rituals, its own etiquette. Reading pornography is reading another kind of text. How to read that text is a ritual of teaching – teaching that may be done either ethically or unethically.

Pornography teaches. It is a genre of formal experimentation: the same limited bodies in the same infinite variations. In queer spaces, it also allows for the possibilities of those bodies in ways that religious or other moral teachings limit. (That can go there? That can do that? That has been done before? That can be done again? That can be done by me? That being done by me enough can open the body enough to allow a new narrative to crawl out? That can be the foundation of an identity?) Pornography enters and presents other possibilities. Pornography makes a moral good a rhetorical argument: another snake, another garden, another tree. Pornography is the head speaking even if the body is detached.

Pornography and pedagogy are better when they avoid moralism, and they risk moralism often. This book is about how I was taught to read and how I was taught to fuck. These intersections of textual and sexual pleasure mirror the crises of pedagogy and pornography against moralism, not for it. I grew up in a religious culture that guarded access to information and access to bodies with equal fervour. The matching of bodies and information. The stories in this book are informational, they are a push back against what I was taught, but they are more comprehensive than that. I wanted to write a book of pornography that also functions as a defence of the pornographic.

Learning, wanting to be taught, being taught, sometimes getting what I wanted, and sometimes being denied – or, even more confusingly, learning the chaos that happens when one gets what they thought they wanted. Vacillating between selves, especially selves connected to body and pleasure, was central to the problem of appetite. Growing up in conservative religious milieus, I knew that admitting what I wanted most was considered toxic. Lessons have mirrors. I learned at once never to have sex, never to masturbate, never to even think or consider the sexual body, but I was sent away to a school where I had more sex than the church elders could have imagined. I learned to never drink, partly because my mother didn't drink at all, partly because my father drank too much, and I eventually learned a stern kind of modesty. I learned to be proper, to have table manners, to send flowers and thank-you notes, and by extension to control my body; and then I learned about the pleasures of too much – too much to eat, too much to drink, too much to fuck, and too much to spend.

I learned how not to read anything that might resemble pornography, and here I am writing pornography, of a sort.

This is a messy history of how I have fucked, and how I have failed to fuck. Talking to friends, I have described it as a post-gender, post-sexuality Prairie Faggot Decameron. It is a pornographic text about my history: how sexual anxiety becomes textual anxiety and how absorbing the pornographic style against my upbringing had equal successes and failures. I want to be blunt about the ambivalences of trauma, and the liminal pleasures of disobedience, in a culture enamoured of rule keeping.

Here, I tell dirty stories, to get to the muck of a life as a reader. Dirty stories about Mormon missionaries, boarding schools, and the backrooms of prairie bars. They are working-class, have the funk of memory: slippery and difficult things. I want to provoke, turn on, offend, and sentimentalize.

These stories happened, but memory and desire are unstable, and so there is a plausible deniability about the whole enterprise.

I keep thinking about Samuel R. Delany's *The Motion of Light in Water* – at turns filthy and lovely, sentimental and haunted, as much about big cities as about small towns. For Delany, it's New York and Texas's Gulf of Mexico; for me, Toronto and the small towns of Alberta. I relate to the romance writer Lorelei James – her knowing how a ranch works as much as the intersection of a cunt and a cock. I like those anonymous digest anthologies that were in the bins of the old Glad Day before it became part–chic café, or the way Dorothy Allison writes about furniture in her short story collection *Trash*. I read Hervé Guibert's *To the Friend Who Did Not Save My Life* for a gossipy roman à clef and ended up wracked by its mourning for a lost lover.

If pornography is a formal moment – the excess of a bodily moment and the containment of that moment – and if pornography is about lessons of etiquette – about being taught, and then by extension teaching others – then what follows is a set of lessons, from people who taught me, sometimes more literally than others. People who had the authority to contain my body, and the brattish, punkish ways that I pushed against that containment.

What follows are a collection of stories about Daddies and what they can do, Daddies and what happens if they are disobeyed, and maybe, pornographically, a depiction of me when I have burst from those lessons – when I refuse being a boy, when I grow up into the ambivalent, genderfucking, post-religious adult that I am.

# Lesson One:
# That Suburban Kid You Fell in Love
# with When You Were Eight

When my dad left my mom he promised he would be back, so I waited a full six months after I turned eight before I was baptized. If you are raised in the Church of Jesus Christ of Latter-day Saints, if you call yourself Mormon, you are supposed to know right from wrong when you are eight years old. You are supposed to know what your sins are, what you have done to anger God or to cause discord with your neighbours. If you are a good eight-year-old, you memorize the thirteenth article of faith, which says: 'We believe in being honest, true, chaste, benevolent, virtuous, and in doing good to all men; indeed, we may say that we follow the admonition of Paul – We believe all things, we hope all things, we have endured many things, and hope to be able to endure all things.'

This suffering and enduring: enough to provide a lifetime of anxiety, a lifetime of fetishes.

What does an eight-year-old know about being honest, about the difference between being true or not? Can an eight-year-old understand chastity?

When I was waiting to be baptized, I started hanging around this eighteen-year-old kid. He was a Southern Albertan Mormon, a better-than-you Mormon, a too-helpful-for-words

Mormon, kind and sweet and smart, sweeter than anyone should feel comfortable with.

Can you fall in love when you are eight?

Most summers, as an act of service, teens would go to the Stake Centre (an administrative location for a collection of wards, which are like parishes; there are between five and twelve wards in a stake), and they would look after us younger kids for the day. I was lonely and awkward, and severely aware when I was being used as a charity case, and I loved it – a needy emotional bottom even then.

Mornings were in the church cultural hall, playing games I was bad at but wasn't made to feel bad at. I was scared of physical contact, of the rough rumble of boys, but this kid didn't feel like a boy to me, didn't feel unsafe.

There was a bowling alley across from the Stake Centre, in the basement of the mall. I asked him if I could get a piggyback ride to the bowling alley from the Stake Centre. It felt like a dangerous request, like I was too old to ask for this, like this would be something I would have to talk to the bishop about. But I saw his spine and his shoulders in perfect perpendicular tension, like an architect's T-square. Innocently, he carried me on his shoulders for two blocks; I curved my body across his neck, tucked my legs into his arms. Even at that young age, I knew the power of that moment, of never being let go, of knowing this was inappropriate, knowing that I wanted more impropriety; no words, no imagination – just, even at eight, a desire to make the pure thing impure, the desire to make the safe thing unsafe.

Around this time, my friends would be baptized by their fathers, and then they would be sealed to their fathers. My father would never be able to baptize me, he would never be able to seal me. In a first moment in a lifetime of disappointments, he couldn't even do the bare minimum, he couldn't even show up. He left my mom about eighteen months before I was to be baptized, to go to Rankin Inlet, as part of a mid-life crisis. He didn't come back to my hometown until he managed to burn out from two jobs and a handful of women.

The Mormons baptize by immersion, and they give the priesthood too young. During the baptisms, they wear these white jumpsuits that cling to the body. Wet jumpsuits leave nothing to the imagination. This imagination included me seeing this innocent eighteen-year-old son of Mom's church friends drowning and lifting me up again, me dying and being reborn in a suburban tiled hot tub, the corpus in a Rotary Hall, and thinking, could I ask him to bring me to the water? I didn't know how to ask – this was a bigger ask than the piggyback ride. Was this a thing that I was allowed to hope for?

Before I could ask, he was sent off on a mission.

Before I was baptized, I had to go to the bishop. The bishop had two roles: a day job and this job, one paid in money and one paid in status. We went to the church office, a bland building near the highway, in the town where I would eventually go to high school. We had an interview and the bishop asked me: did I lie, did I steal, did I say unkind words to my sister, did I take what wasn't mine? I told him I lied a little, and once I took something that wasn't mine (cookies out of the cookie jar). I told him that I said mean things to my sister every so often, and that I wasn't as helpful as I could be to my mom. I told him that I was angry at my dad. I didn't tell him about the kid.

The LDS is led spiritually by very young men, and also by very old men. When you are eight you are baptized. When you are twelve you are a deacon and allowed to pass the sacrament on Sunday. When you are fourteen you are a teacher and allowed to bless the sacrament that the deacons pass. When you are sixteen you are encouraged to go out and visit other LDS families once a month, and when you are eighteen you are allowed to bless, to set apart, to heal, and to go on missions. Between twelve and sixteen you are allowed to go to the temple. You can baptize people who have died and gone to spirit prison; in spirit prison, the deceased can decide to accept the gospel and be baptized.

This was if you were a boy or presented as a boy. *The Family: A Proclamation to the World*, revealed to the prophet and head of the church, then distributed and read in each ward when I was thirteen, said that there were only ever boys and girls; I didn't have the language yet, had not read enough, to know that I would eventually become 'not a boy' or 'not a girl.' The first break with being a boy, then, was being passed into boyhood, to do these eternally sacred tasks, and realizing that I didn't belong, that I wasn't going to be allowed in. My family would not last forever anyway: my dad wasn't a member of the church, and then he left. My first real textual irony, maybe my first bleak reading, was being forced to sing, at the age of eight, a saccharine hymn to mainstream heteropatriarchy called 'Daddy's Homecoming (I'm So Glad When Daddy Comes Home),' or to sing the song 'Families Can Be Together Forever,' when I knew that I didn't have a family, and they wouldn't stay together. Daddy wasn't coming home, and families never stay together.

There was cruelty in the church, attempts at censoring, genuine anger, but these didn't compare to the moment when

I realized that the text everyone was singing did not describe a state to which I would be welcomed – that was the cruelty I integrated.

In adulthood, the hardest conversation I ever had with my mother was about her disappointment – not with me or the church, but with the strangeness of the world – that her two queer children would never be sealed, that she spent half a century as a Mormon on this promise of eternal family and then had her children reject it. The irony is that other possibilities – like that gender might not be essential, that there were spaces for me that were not male or female – and maybe my first break with the church, came from that same document. *The Family: A Proclamation to the World* gave me other possibilities, other ways forward. Before the proclamation, nothing was ever talked about, and not talking about things means that you cannot imagine possiblities. By stating clearly that other genders or other sexualities could exist, it allowed me to imagine possibilities previously veiled.

It's like this pamphlet called *For the Strength of Youth*. Given to each early adolescent, it presented every viable way not to express lust, in a sly, nodding style. It was not supposed to give ideas, but it also gave enough information that you were sufficiently castigated for crossing a line. The problem is that it told me about things that I might want, things I had never considered wanting. Just as the declaration about families suggested to me that other genders and other sexual identities were possible, the pamphlet suggested other sexual practices were possible.

It talked of women's backs and arms in unflattering terms, of strapless dresses, spaghetti straps, sundresses, and evening dresses. It suggested that the back or the arms were not erotic sites. Well, this is not true – the back, the shoulder, the arm are all erotic, all sexually possible in ways that they tried to argue against. The pamphlet argued aesthetics when it was talking about morality. It intertwined both in my head – also, that modest dress was erotic, that covering up didn't take the hunger or the desire away. Then it listed the forbidden behaviours. Men having sex with men, however, was a lust that was not even named, so beyond the pale that it was not even considered. Women were portrayed as those who seduced, who took advantage of young men. Officially: 'Necking, petting, intimacies, and improprieties of every kind should not be indulged in at any time in dating or in courtship. Love and affection are precious, and virtue must never be placed in jeopardy.'

All that made me want to do was indulge in everything – not to take advantage, but to find someone who was willing to neck or pet with me. Then the second half of that sentence, that hungry, ambivalent sentence, the 'should' slithering out from this thicket of prohibition. Just as I knew that I would never be sealed to my mother or my sister, that the generation before me would never be sanctified, I knew that I would never have a second generation, that I would not court or marry or have a baby – not that I could articulate it like that.

The gap between what one wanted, what one could have, and the prohibition and the guidelines: this policing of desire grew large and dark in my thinking. But the church was cruel, and the cruelty wasn't always soft. You would talk to the bishop at twelve, or fourteen, or sixteen, about the next level of power. In a moment of mutual awkwardness, he would ask you about adult sins, about that jerking off you weren't supposed to do, the jerking off that would cut you out from the top levels of heaven. They believed that hetero jerking off led to pornography, to sexual appetites, and even perhaps to premarital sex. It was so overwhelming that it would slop over to other categories. The line between straight jerking off and queer jerking off was foggier and more conceptual. Straight jerking off was a gateway to other sodomitical practices; jerking off itself was a kind of sodomy ...

Maybe they got the power of desire to overwhelm a little bit correct.

All the boys who I wanted to fuck me between twelve and fifteen, they were the nice boys, the genial boys, the boys who would give you a ride to youth group, the boys who would pray for you and thank you when you did chores with them for service days, the boys who pretended that you weren't queer and you weren't crazy. Jerking off to those boys was like eating vanilla soft serve, smooth and sweet and uncomplex. Jerking off about them now is an act of nostalgia, like adults going to Disneyland, or watching Disney cartoons on Saturday morning – an act of ambitious memory over anything real.

I still jerk off to thoughts of that first boy. He is my sweetest and most tender memory. I never told anyone – the bishops who interviewed me for worthiness, my parents, my eventual priests – that in moments of stress or grief, when I want to return to a moment of tenderness, where a body could meet another body, I think of that young man carrying me on his shoulders. That tenderness has eros, and that tenderness has something more – an absence of cruelty perhaps.

Wrapping my body around his torso, having him carry me, being brought from a place of sanctity to a place of leisure, the cruelty of the church disappears, then returns.

In 1976, Boyd K. Packer, an LDS theologian and church elder, delivered a talk during the biannual international meeting of Mormons. It was directed at boys. It was still being delivered and distributed when I was a kid. The talk told us our bodies were holy, but the holiness rested on regulation, i.e., constant surveillance. Surveil yourself and surveil others. Nothing to be touched, nothing seen, nothing adored as much as the Lord – but the Lord without ecstasy.

The talk slips into an industrial metaphor. I grew up in a landscape of industrial farming and chemical plants, a West of factories and the production of food and fuel for the rest of the country. The metaphors that we used to describe our bodies were borrowed from metaphors that we used to describe these industries. Alberta was a farm and oil economy, and the LDS church had vast tracts of agricultural land throughout the mountain West. The dominant metaphor of the church, and of growing up on the land, was hoping for a boom in the middle of a bust, and trying to find a regulatory system to ride out the bad years. When church leaders spoke the words of Packer, the body held the memory of that boom-and-bust cycle. The only way to properly have sex, to properly regulate, was in marriage. Packer took this to heart: he had ten children.

The industrial metaphor is explained over several hundred words, in a complex and overwrought way. There is an anxiety in how he speaks of boys' bodies. For him, a body is a factory, and in early adolescence the factory begins production. The Lord modulates the production via nocturnal emissions – though he doesn't use that phrase exactly, nor the euphemism 'wet dreams,' that is what Packer is getting at. He intones about how masturbating speeds up the means of production, making semen less robust, less viable for what it's intended for: namely, making children.

Again, the idea that masturbating gives you so much power that the simple act of pleasure can break you is part of it. The church owned these vast sugar beet farms in Arizona, Alberta, and Utah, millions of sugar beets, industrially farmed and processed. The sweetness squeezed out of the beets by a giant industrial machine. Breeding and cross-breeding and breeding again for the sweetest of the vegetables, and then new technology for the release. In agriculture, the 'oversupply of (a) substance' was the key to prosperity. But maybe there was over-abundance in other matters too – I remember sitting in the back of the chapel at eight or nine years old and seeing these families of more than half a dozen and thinking that itself was overproduction. Abundance itself wasn't a crisis – only if it was the wrong kind of abundance. Being a man was excess contained, excess controlled – being something else (a queer, not a man, a sissy, a decadent, a fag) was excess that refused control, was being someone who enjoys the factory so much they speed it past overproduction.

However, the florid desires – the fantasies, thoughts, and hunger – could be their own act of creation. Wanting a lover, working for ways to find that lover, having that lover, keeping that lover: all acts of creation. Especially in this land of repression.

There is a coda to this talk that is not in the printed copy. In it, Packer tells the story of a missionary approaching his companion for sex and being punched out for asking – in the words of the talk, 'laying him flat out.' Told as a joke, with a literal punch line, to a collection of mostly adults, the list of acts that are allowed is made clear: wet dreams are fine, masturbation is less fine, sex outside of marriage with women is a problem that can be fixed, what was called euphemistically 'same-sex desire' will result in you being attacked, and that attack can be the subject of a mediocre comedy routine.

Packer's lecture was documented in a tract, given to me when I was a young adult by a man whose calling was to take care of the spiritual needs of boys. Its cover had a pencil-drawn illustration of an earnest boy. (If there's a pencil sketch of a clean-cut, earnest young man in 1976 on the cover, it's got to be religious agit prop or gay porn, a pamphlet about the military, a tight little pick-up scene – a pick-up for Jesus, a pick-up cock, or a pick-up of both if you were lucky, a bit of a tender perversion about all this wholesomeness.)

Reading Neil LaBute's plays about masculinity in my twenties, after I had left the church, put all this in context. LaBute, a graduate of the church-run Brigham Young University and, for decades, a faithful Mormon, writes plays that function as essays of cruelty. They are texts that recognize that the picking up of converts and the picking up of men feel the same – that the pamphlet had two parallel audiences, that they required you to believe both that you were wanted and that you wanted others. I could see myself as the person being picked up, for sex or for religious ardour. I could see myself picking up less clearly. The tension between picking up and being picked up was central to learning how to be a good Mormon, and eventually how to be effective at queer sex. The double lesson stuck with me all the way up to the Eaton Centre bathroom.

LaBute is a straight boy who is in love with other straight boys, who writes about the sexual possibilities of gay men in dark corners. He still thinks that the moral consequences of dark corners mean that it is impossible to find them redemptive. But the people who go into the dark park shadows, or feral washrooms, or the wilds beside highway traffic, go as a kind of act of moral bravery. They go and then they go again and they meet other people. They craft communities. They learn patterns of desire. They go despite being robbed or broken apart or beaten or destroyed.

When I was seventeen, on occasion I went to the bathroom on the fourth floor of the Edmonton Eaton Centre downtown. It was hidden at the end of an abandoned corridor. There was a creaky door, then a long, carpeted hallway, then another creaky door. It was the perfect bathroom for public sex. But the cops knew, and then it was renovated: the hallway was taken out, the doors replaced, security guards were hired, and the place went away. The bathroom had multiple uses, and then it had one use. Before the renovation, before the cops, before feeling like I belonged, I remember having those respectability-minded gays tell the same stories as the churches when I was growing up, warning me that those spaces were dangerous … that the hunger and the danger are fed by the same spring and satiated by a mutual resolve. The hunger grows in the dark, wilder and rawer than any ritual; even learning how to publicly cruise has an etiquette. Learning it well, eventually, is like knowing how to use an escargot fork.

I had the shit kicked out of me in high school once or twice. It was never the Mormon boys who did it. Boys together are never safer than boys apart. When a neighbourhood boy you want to fuck slams his hand into you, that becomes a fucking. The catharsis of a boot to the back near the kidney, the half catharsis of a cock through my lips, the dull ache of hunger not fulfilled. When a boy who you want to enter shoves you, it becomes like a cock shoving into your asshole. When a boy hisses *faggot* at you, the clarity is more precise than ever. When a boy calls you a cocksucker, well, that's just a Boy Scout merit badge. No one has the courage to say *yes*, and the courage atrophies, then rots into self-loathing. The boys become men; the men teach the boys.

The failure to be a boy, the failure to be a man, is the failure to both teach and be taught.

# Lesson Two:
# On the Sanctification of Violence

Neil LaBute's *Your Friends and Neighbors* is a riff on the Restoration comedy *The Country Wife* by William Wycherley. It is a play for an era when pleasure was restored from Puritan roots, a play about marriage, city ethics and country ethics, the power of sex, and the problem of pleasure. LaBute wrote this for Aaron Eckhart, a fellow Brigham Young University student and devout church member.

LaBute surgically extracted the cruelty from Wycherley. In LaBute's text, there is a scene in a locker room. Three friends, Barry, Cary, and Jerry, are talking about their greatest lay. Cary is an obstetrician played in the film version by Jason Patric, Jerry is a professor of Restoration lit played by Ben Stiller, and Barry is a sad schlump played by Aaron Eckhart. We know that Barry is a schlump because his wife doesn't want to fuck him. Barry's wife is being fucked by Jerry. Barry can get hard for his wife and Jerry can't for his.

Cary leads the conversation to the greatest fuck they have ever had. Barry says, 'My wife.' We don't rest on this at all. We don't spend serious time thinking about what exactly it means that the best fuck you have ever had might be with your wife. Partly because LaBute spends so much time disparaging women, and partly because Barry does not seem to enjoy fucking his wife. Cary confesses his best fuck. He was a student in boarding school, and there was a younger student, Timmy, who they all hated. Five men systematically raped the student at school. They took turns. Cary talks about how tight Timmy was, and how he squeezed his ass, enfolding it onto Cary's cock. It's the best lay that Cary ever had because he was in control, maybe also because of an esprit de corps between the five students that let Cary finally get what he wanted. The confession happens in a steam room – how easy would it be for Barry to reach over and grasp Cary under his towel? There is something accurate here, that one knows what one is by what one isn't, that one is forced to declare identity by hostile forces, and that there is something deeply sexy about being forced to say out loud what you think secretly. All the boys and men who pushed their hands or mouths or cocks or tongues toward me, all the shoves into the mud and the ritual humiliation deepened my own queerness, my own refusals, my own gender – and my own desire to eroticize the violence's impact.

LaBute made a handful of movies and plays with Eckhart; for the first half of their careers, Eckhart was effectively a muse for the writer and director. A straight man obsessed with another straight man writes a cluster of works for him. The works he made centre on the sexual cruelty of men – sometimes men to women, sometimes men to men about women. The cruelty mattered more than the sex, or maybe men's sexuality seemed inextricable from cruelty. LaBute's comedies of manners are comedies of sex, his comedies of sex are comedies of cruelty. All centred on Eckhart, this blond all-American man, as subject of gaze: an obsession.

LaBute might never have wanted to fuck Eckhart, but I think he wanted his social ease, and wanted to be him, and wanted to humiliate him for that. The closest LaBute ever got, the sexiest he ever got, and his best work about boys playing in power, was in *Your Friends and Neighbors*, a movie that featured actual queer people, but queer people who were not allowed autonomy – they were stripped of that autonomy in a way that the straight boys were not. LaBute's work up to this point featured sexual violence sublimated among white men. In this film, he expands a bit – there are women present, and some of those women sleep with each other.

Thinking about power, the church, and bodies, how LaBute reclaims an eighteenth-century comedy of manners for a twentieth-century discourse of cruelty, I am reminded of the Marquis de Sade and his central irony. He wrote about liberty – and was claimed as the great libertine, in the French Revolution and afterward. Reading his pornographic novels, like *Justine* or *The 120 Days of Sodom*, I note the same acts occurring over and over again. In his unfinished *120 Days*, a group of aristocrats retreat to a castle in the Black Forest. There, thirty-six subjects are told to perform explicit ritual acts – ritual acts whose sexual power gave the practices a name, and later an identity. The eros does not come from abandon but the exact opposite – restriction. The book was only discovered in 1904 and translated in the 1920s ... so, oddly, it is a twentieth-century document.

In French porn after Sade – in Alain Robbe-Grillet's late erotic novels or Pauline Réage's *Story of O* – there is a similar, careful attention to the manners of the encounters; the landscape the manners occur in and the politics of it count as much or more than a cock entering an asshole. For American inheritors of the tradition – see Dennis Cooper, or Samuel R.

Delany's porn novels like *Hogg* – there is a reflection of this reflection, there is a different kind of order, but an order that could be carefully documented via the proper charting. There is something about how the locked chamber of the château (for Robbe-Grillet) or the prison cell (for Jean Genet), truck cab (for Delany in *Hogg*) or suburban home (for Cooper), all match the locked chamber of the heart, and the interlocking of bodies. For LaBute, in *Your Friends and Neighbors*, the sex is less explicit, but the talking is as explicit, and he notices how the erotic charge of Mormon Utah and WASP New York have that same interlocking tendency, that same rage, that same quality of good manners gone stale or rotten.

In this tradition, where everything is predetermined and programmatic, early LaBute refuses the Mormon obsession with agency as a gift from God. I am thinking especially of a suite of one-acts called *bash: latterday plays*. In the middle one, *a gaggle of saints*, the plotting points to this problem.

There's a party at the Plaza Hotel. Two couples, who are juniors at a college in Boston, go to the Plaza for a church party – we don't know which church. They're well-dressed, formal, the men in Perry Ellis tuxedos. The party ends badly. A boy named John and a girl named Sue tell the story, and so it's a tale about what is unknown in the mutual retelling. As is typical for LaBute, a straight boy enacts ritual cruelty on a straight girl for an audience of other straight boys.

Early on in the play, there's a moment that foreshadows the impending violence: Sue and John excitedly tell their friends the details of how John pricked his finger putting on a corsage. The couple goes back and forth, interrupting and finishing each other's sentences: Susan uses the word *prick*, she marvels at how the blood, a red spot on a white shirt, excites her in a strange way. The writing, about violence and sex, staining and capital, is not subtle but it's effective.

Blood is exciting, and disorder is exciting, and getting close enough to get someone to bleed is exciting, and the blood – maybe that everything collapses in this act of bloodletting, the intimacy of a corsage and pinprick, and the bleeding of a ruptured hymen, and a fist in the right place. The excitement of cruel boys joshing in the corner of the cultural hall, the basketball games in Walmart cotton button-ups and polyester pants, the tussle of a play fight that might turn into a real fight, the copper at the back of your throat, self-inflicted, when biting cheek or tongue, or the bright red against skin when picking a little too much …

I recognize in LaBute the sanctified excuses for violence and the excitement that rises in the throat when the violence approaches. The violence is implied, coming from a hidden place, and the violence is explicit, connected to the structure of the church itself. It is not like the passage in Luke, about how 'what is done in the dark will be brought to the light,' what is done in the light is also done in the dark. When I went away to school, this sadistic/masochistic doubling was clear; reading LaBute later made me realize that it also existed in hetero marriages, in non-religious spaces.

Back to *a gaggle of saints*. A group of boys walk to Central Park, where they find two men making out. The two men's kissing is said to resemble a film with Clark Gable, a very New York moment, the kind of thing that occurs after other pleasures in the city – here, either the symphony or some foreign film. John imagines queerness as another symptom of restless urbanity.

He follows one of the men into a cruising area. He wants to punish the man for having what he does not have … and so he does. John's friends are gone, the man who is cruising separates from his date, and then it's John and the man being cruised in the same punk house, while Sue talks about pleasant, lovely times in the hotel with the rest of her friends …

Through the mention of the symphony or foreign films, LaBute implies that gay sex in public is cosmopolitan, excluded from him. Queerness owns the night, and queerness is all kinds of sophisticated pleasures – even Clark Gable was urbane and thus queer. I recognized this, first in my own life, not finding a text for it, and then reading *bash* in my early twenties in a carrel on the fifth floor of the Toronto Reference Library – closer to New York than small-town Alberta, time and space collapsed.

There are moments when two cocks or a cock and a mouth can find each other in the dark, and after an encounter or two, they return to conventional lives. Separating the body from desire. Queerness exists when the commitment to a hunger becomes too wild, too all-consuming, and a deliberate choice is made: to break from heterosexuality. LaBute notes that the desire to bash comes from an anxiety. It's a recognition that the break itself can be violent – the explosion after a life of repression has shrapnel.

# Lesson Three:
## On the Absence of Daddies

I grew up in Fort Saskatchewan, Alberta. I attended kinder-garten at a school near downtown, but it was torn down. I was sent to French immersion, but flunked out, and was sent to an English-language public school from Grade 3 to Grade 6. The report cards from those years repeated the same phrases: bright but not working hard enough; or disorganized; or messy; or not living up to my potential. I then was sent to a boarding school in Grades 7 and 8. I lived in two houses. The big house disappeared when my father left, and then came the small house. My mom taught for thirteen hours a day, and so before and after school, I would go to other people's houses, or I would go to after-school clubs. These early houses, this early child care – some were pious, and some were rough, and they taught me. I remember reading old *Ladies Home Journals* in one baby-sitter's room, waiting for everyone to get up and start their day, learning about the failures of domesticity in theory and practice. I remember watching those eighties movies, with their gratuitous showing of women's tits, and watching the tits, watch-ing the grown-ups in the house, who had told us about the tits, and wondering what was next. The babysitters, mothers of rough sons, employed by my soft mother so they could have extra money, would show me these movies and be delighted that I was priggish. They saw this kid who would prefer to read or sleep before school, while they enjoyed the scandal, the low comedy, of *Ski School* or *Porky's*.

The sons of these people seemed adult, even at twelve or thirteen. Their appetites were hungrier, and they were slyer. They rarely wore shirts from June to September. They had brothers or sisters who were wiser. Once, one of their sisters showed me her full bush when I asked what sex was; another time, walking through a park, I saw another sister fucking her boyfriend on a knoll.

More than once, these boys would push against me. They would push their bodies into me. Or onto me. They would pile on top; dogpile, they called it. The dogpiling had an alpha quality. Boys would push their hands onto my chest, push their hip into my hip, they would choke my neck with callused hands, shove my nose into pits and ass – they knew their bodies were disgusting, and I wanted to be fully absorbed into the disgust of their bodies.

I wanted to submit to all kinds of bodies. All of this was my desire to have my body under the control of another body. It was its own kind of masochism. Even at eight I knew that my body could not be sanctified, even at twelve I knew that my body was not my own, that it had to be controlled by other people, mostly older men. When I was five, I was brought into the city once a month and asked to perform monotonous tasks, to train a body that was already unruly. From that time onward, once a week I was sent away from class and brought to a small room behind the gym, where I would spend an hour bouncing a red ball against a concrete wall, trying to improve my hand-eye coordination. I spent six months playing soccer without once getting a kick on the goal. I spent four months playing

T-ball. One time at bat, I tried to hit the ball on the tee a few dozen times, never connecting. My grandfather, one Christmas, spent two hours after dinner trying to teach me how to use my fork. My grandmother, over several years, tried to teach me how to eat toast with butter and jam. I was fat, I was clumsy, my unruly body broke objects and other people around me, and there was a fear that I would break myself. So they sent me away.

I learned that my body was this dangerous feral thing, to be moulded by touch, by violence, and eventually by desire. I was sent away to make me a boy, in order to make me a man; aping the boy, aping the man, a set of ambitions that were shattered, then reassembled, then shattered, then assembled yet again. Everything about my identity was set through acts of refusal – I was no longer a boy, no longer a woman, no longer a Mormon, not quite gay, definitely not straight, ungraceful, my clumsy and fat body against its own social order. The cracks of identity would break me apart, leave me to pick up the pieces – but the pieces were smaller, less coherent, and less consistent. I would have to learn to craft personae from these fragile, fractured parts – the wholeness, not the parts themselves, but the capricious light that shined through them.

I remember one afternoon in late spring or early summer, in the complex of townhouses that we lived in. I was playing with another boy, getting into some kind of mischief. It was warm but not too hot, and eventually, he was bored. He invited me back to his house. His condo was bigger than ours, and two storeys, whereas ours had only one storey. He brought me to his small room, dominated by a hand-me-down king-bed suite. On the bookshelf at the top of the bed, there was a collection of encyclopedias. We lay down on the bed together, hip to hip, as he showed me scientific illustrations of anatomy – I didn't have the language, in that dusty room, to ask him to show in flesh what we were seeing in theory.

There were other occasions where I saw more flesh. I was friends with the son of a wealthy man. The mother was surgically perfect, ivory skin, breasts a masterpiece of the medical arts. In an Oedipal moment, my friend and I would go back to his room, and he would show me issues of *Playboy* or *Penthouse*. Two boys on the same bed, again hip to hip, ignoring our growing cocks. There is this triangle of queer perversion here – of regulation. Wanting to jerk off, wanting to watch my friend jerk off, maybe even wanting to touch my friend in his room, not knowing why his immediate family was rich and my immediate family was poor, not quite understanding the difference between his money and my mother's lack of money. I would think about his lumpen, ugly father fucking his perfect mother and never quite know exactly how that happened. Though now, as an adult, I know that ignoring our growing cocks was ignoring a kind of erotic potential.

Later that summer, Grade 6, with another boy with a single mother (a smaller apartment than mine), and the kid with the *Playboy*s. The single mother's son had a VHS copy of hard-core pornography, the kind that I was warned would be the end of my soul. His mother was at work, and he told us he had something he wanted to show us. He went to the top of his closet and got a black tape out of a box. He had borrowed it from a brother or an older cousin. These three boys, who hadn't sorted out how they felt, watching this ...

Watching the screen, flopped in a dusty apartment, built on top of a shop whose purpose changed every six months.

Fast-forward to waiting for a brother to show up and reclaim his property – waiting to be beat up, or even more exciting, perhaps, waiting to be taught, just starting to masturbate, and at that moment, wanting to do it better, wanting to exchange knowledge …

It never happened. I slipped my hands under my jeans, the movie stopped, everyone stared, I was pushed out of the house and told not to come back. I didn't even get the pleasure of a beat-down.

I was a feral kid trying not to be feral, a scared kid, pushing his fear into explosions of violence – of cruel words, of pulled hair, of screaming, of significant material damage, even of fire-setting. Manipulating, scrapping, pushing … Dad had left for the Arctic. Mom was a single parent, with too little money, working thirteen-hour days teaching and taking on extra work. Part of the feralness was being bored; part of it was not knowing what to do next.

# Lesson Four:
# Restriction and Expansion in
# Missionary Territories Among
# Missionary Bodies

When I was eighteen, the church thought they were going to lose me, and so they sent missionaries to get me to come back to the Lord. That's an act that looks an awful lot like seduction. They invited me to play basketball on their off days, to go door-to-door knocking, to go to special church services, and eventually, they invited me to their home. I thought maybe we were friends, though the ulterior motive was always present.

Mormon missionaries are never supposed to leave each other's side – practice for marriage, for more proper kinds of love. They sleep in the same room, pray, and eat together. Now it's all social media, Facebook chats, and TikTok dances, but back then, the only connection to home was a call on Christmas and another on Mother's Day, and one day a week for playing basketball with other missionaries. They are bored and lonely; it's boring and lonely. Maybe I made them less lonely.

Mormons mythologize the West, both in the manifest destiny sense, and in the Joan Didion ennui sense; this mythology is deepened on missions – they are genuinely international, but more often than not, the missions move across the American West, Utah to Idaho or Idaho to California, or Arizona to Alberta, but it was rare to see a missionary pair that wasn't at least half Utahn.

Both of the eighteen-year-old Elders were American: one from the near west and one from the far west. Far West was the small wiry one. Near West looked like he surfed, played football. If Far West was smart and small, Near West was big and dumb. He looked right out of central casting. He looked a little like Harold's gift in *The Boys in the Band* or like one of the *Boys in the Sand* or one of Harry Bush's *Hard Boys*, or Moose – not in *Riverdale*, the hip remake, but in the *Archie* comic books. We never called them by their names. Far West was tight and compact with a nervous energy, smart and constrained. The missionaries before and after him were so compliant that they seemed stupid. Near West never seemed stupid. He seemed accidentally mean, one of those selfish boys who you couldn't ask for what you wanted, and you didn't know what you wanted, and so you just kind of wandered around him.

When they are eighteen, Mormons are given underwear, which covers everything from the knee to the neck. There is a hole in the front to use the washroom. The sacred symbols of the church are above the left breast, nearest the heart. I never get the underwear. I get a lifetime of wanting instead.

Here is why.

It's my birthday, I am eighteen. I am invited over to the missionaries' apartment for dinner and cake. Dinner is chili; cake is Duncan Hines. I am not supposed to be here, they are making an exception for our small closeness. They pick me up, and I suspect they will drop me off. I feel special. I'm in the front seat, it's a Honda or something like it – beige or grey. It's the blandest way to get from my mom's place to their place, for the blandest meal, with the blandest men, and I've never felt more special.

There isn't a lot of conversation on the car ride over, not much chatter, and the radio can't be turned on, it'd be too secular. I can still plot the road out of the townhouse complex: left onto the main drag, past the grocery stores and shopping plazas, turn left at the old railway station from before they shut the passenger trains down, right at a cluster of mid-seventies mid-level apartments, smaller and shabbier than the missionaries', though not by much.

The missionaries' place is a small two-bedroom apartment on the edge of the hill going down to a park by the river. Built in the 1970s, part of a collection of starter rentals for shift workers before the town decided it was going to be a suburb. Two bedrooms, living room, tiny kitchen, smaller bathroom. I give up who I am in order to access a couple of hours in a shitty apartment with people who don't love me but are really good at faking it. Near West leaves to get milk. We need milk for cake, and we need milk for the chili – he made it spicy just for me – though I know that it's a cliché, getting milk in this way. This leaves Far West and me alone for a solid fifteen minutes or so.

The bathroom at the missionaries' place has two wallet-sized cards taped up in their shower, one of Jesus and one of the articles of faith. It's so that when you are tempted to jerk off, you could look at Mormon Jesus: perfect, Aryan, clad in a red robe. You could look at what you were supposed to be doing, and you would clean up quickly. Kind of like when you were a kid and you were told that more than three shakes and you were playing with yourself.

In the bathroom, pissing, remembering not to shake it more than three times. I have my cock in my hand half-hard, thinking about being in that space, thinking about those two boys, barely older than me, in charge of my future. I think less about individual acts, less about wanting to fuck them or have them fuck me, and more about this space, crossing the threshold, being welcomed into a house that I am not supposed to be in. The eroticism of access, of finally being allowed inside, and learning that people pitying you gets you that access.

Walking out of the bathroom, facing Far West on the couch, suit still on. (He wore suits sometimes from Twice But Nice, the local thrift store; he wore suits his momma bought him before he came to this suburb.) His cock is jutting out from the white polyester drawers, flagpole stiff, and I stand at attention, then kneel at attention. I have to pretend that this is new to me, that this is my first cock, that I have never thought about this cock and this mouth, the half-hard-on from the bathroom grown to regimental size.

I engulf his cock – his balls still tucked under – not knowing what to do with the whole package, worried that Near West will come back, flummoxed by the temple garments; it is just me and the cock and the open mouth and something like prayer …

And he is bucking, lifting his ass, his glans on the back of my throat – too quick for him to cum, too quick for me to see the seal above his left tit, half a task, done badly – when Near West catches us, in flagrante delicto. He drops the milk, four litres across the cheap parquet. Not to put too fine a point on it, but this is the cum shot, transmitted, and translated across material. This is the surprise I got.

I wonder what Far West's chest felt like, I wonder what it would feel like to spread my hand across it, my thumb and pinkie pulling at a nipple; I wonder how it would feel to kiss him, scruff against scruff.

Two weeks before Far West's cock was in my mouth, the Elders went to my warren of a downstairs bedroom with three black garbage bags and threw out everything that was demonic, that they thought was making me unhappy: Dad's drug books from the 1960s, cassettes of Nirvana and NIN, Anne Rice vampire novels, a whole run of *Details* from the mid-nineties, three black garbage bags of intergenerational demimonde in the dumpster at the end of the condo complex. And it was supposed to make me feel happier.

The milk-spiller calls his boss. His boss comes with his wife. The wife drives me home in a nice, newish, modest sedan. I look out the window, through the traffic, the seventies apartments, the gas stations – she doesn't talk, the radio isn't on, new snow falls on old snow. She doesn't come in and make small conversation with my mom. Her demeanour isn't one of disgust or horror or anger. Her face is frozen in politeness, or exhaustion, or maybe both.

I next saw the Elders, or at least one of them, accidentally. Far West was waiting for his worthiness interview, and I was waiting for mine – his was late, I came early, and we saw each other in the hallway, too quiet or too polite to say anything. He was sent way up north. They asked me a lot of questions, then they asked me to leave. The Elder said that I had seduced him; I said the Elder and I had a good time.

Maybe both were true, but I like to think that he seduced me.

Last I heard, he had a wife, children, a good job, and a strong faith.

There is a narrative about repression, and a narrative about not making choices. The potential of that blow job, the story of that interruption, was the last moment for me – an awareness of the deepening fracture between me and Salt Lake. For him, from what I know, the life he had foreordained was too valuable to break up.

I wonder if he is on Grindr. I wonder if he is one of those men whose wife thinks the ride home is half an hour longer than it actually is. I wonder if he ever gets lonely. I wonder what he thinks about in moments when he no longer keeps himself modest.

I want to finish the incomplete task. It's all I have ever wanted. Him and me, in the bed he shares with his wife, on the couch where he reads to his kids. I want to see him out of the garments. Imagine it in August, his family away for the day. He knows I am in town on some research trip, he invites me back to his place – I take the train, I take a cab, it winds through similar McMansions, the same buff colour as the sand and the pavement. I knock on the door, he's expecting me.

He still wears the suit he wore when he was eighteen. The house is clean and a little shaggy. He invites me in, pulls the shades down. He offers me a soda from the fridge. We make small talk about work. I begin to think that he's forgotten why I am there. He's a good host, ice in the glass, soda over ice. He takes off the suit jacket; I can see the white garments underneath the white T-shirt.

The wife will be home soon, the kids will be home soon, the small talk will continue unabated. He loosens his tie. I walk over to the couch and sit next to him. I nestle into him. I behave more bravely now than I did then, I function as bravely as he did when I was eighteen. I want him to know that he taught me how to be brave: to be an adult is to be brave, to be an adult is to ask for what I want.

In my fantasy, in this corrective desire, in this imaginary moment, I reach over and undo a shirt button, then two, then climb over him, face him. His shirt is just a plain white tee, absent of the signs of a sacred garment. His hair peeks out from the cotton. He is quick and efficient with the shedding of his clothes – a task to be accomplished. I lean back as he finishes the shirt, I get off his lap as he is shedding his pants. His underwear separates from his T-shirt – does his wife know about this lack of sanctity? Is this lack of sanctity for me? Imagining him strip quickly, I still take my time.

In the living room with these giant windows, almost visible from the street, anonymous and dull, finally my fingers stretching his tits, finally whole palms clasping his chest hair. My teeth moving south, mutual cocks straining, hands and mouths, angrily, fiercely consuming each other's flesh, and the decades of waiting, cumming mattering less than finally closing the circle.

I have learned to take care of Daddy, Daddy has learned to take care of me, maybe I can prove it.

A good Daddy absorbs the erotics of care: wipe away tears, wipe away cum, spilled milk, or spilled tea. Cleaning up a mess and making a mess and cleaning up again.

# Lesson Five:
# The Farmer Teaches the City Kid
# How to Be a Boy

**M**ormons believe the father is head of the household and boys are heads of the household if fathers are gone. There were people who came once a month to fatherless families to ask if they needed help, to read scripture, pray, give a brief moral lesson, and then move on to the next house. The lessons were about how to be a father, how to wield power softly. These people were concerned about the boy not finding love or finding love in the wrong places.

I think that meant finding a girl and going off with that girl too young, or it meant not going on a mission, or losing worthiness. There were bits in the manual about being an ordinary gay person. There was little about any queerness or gender that went beyond the borders. Central in their teachings was the anxiety of spilling past righteousness, not maintaining the careful lines, and the more anxious they were to teach me, the more and more I wanted to lavish my excesses on them.

The fathers of the church I grew up in treated me like I was their child. They were kind, and I was lonely – and I wanted all of their kindness to be more complex than pity. They took me on drives through the country, invited me to home-cooked dinners, drove me to out-of-town pilgrimages, and all I thought about was how I wanted them to take care of other appetites, other desires.

The dads didn't understand what Freud meant by transference. Sometimes they would take me camping and I would walk into the woods and stare back at the campground, thinking of them; sometimes they would take me through the McDonald's drive-through and we would eat cones on their car hood on the edge of town, practising on the ice cream cone, never practising on the dad, the dad and Daddy dialectic.

———

There was a man in our county, a man of much influence, who volunteered time to work with young people. Let's call him the Farmer. The Farmer loved Jesus, the Farmer loved the church, the Farmer had a handful of kids. Even if we called each other Brother or Sister, he was a Daddy.

The church is in the basement of the 1970s public library, the washrooms are huge, with brash fluorescent lighting. I go in to piss between the first and second meeting. He is in there, angry at his kid for not finishing up, or not behaving in sacrament meeting. The Farmer unloops his belt and takes it into his hand, cracking it as a promise and a threat. Scared, I look over to him, and he looks over to me, gives me a sly smile. It's a threat I cannot quite determine.

I want the Farmer to send his kids home, and in the five minutes or so before someone else comes in, I want him to bend me over the sink and lash my ass with his leather belt. I want him to make sure to use the buckle, I want his hand, made firm with manual labour, to guide my ass in such a way that the belt makes maximum impact. I want all the people to melt away and for him to use that hand to grab my cock, I want him to press his entire body into mine, hard-on pushing through cheap polyester dress pants. I want him to ask if I am ready to be a good boy, I want him to hiss the phrase *Have you stopped your nonsense?* I never want to stop my nonsense.

Early in high school, we were all supposed to go camping in Central Alberta: the Farmer, a Scout leader, and half a dozen other people, boys and leaders. I spent five weeks before that day imagining everything I could do to the Farmer. I could sleep next to him, I could hear him sleep, I could imagine us swimming, though that would require taking off garments and I couldn't imagine swimming with the garments off. We could go hiking. I could taste or smell his rank sweat, his thick odour. His kid got sick. We never went camping.

We did go swimming, with other boys, with another leader or two. The Farmer changed quickly and didn't shower before slipping into the pool. Sherwood Park, out of town, one of those rec centres built as an example of civic pride. We are all playing an aggressive game of water polo, and I want to touch more than others, grabbing, pushing, pulling not just flesh but the accidental-on-purpose grasp of swimming trunks as well. Later, as we change, he is standing in front of me. I am unsubtle in my looks, so he moves away to the next bench, shielding his body. I leave quickly, he holds back. When we get back to the van, he castigates everyone. He stayed longer in the change room because there was a father who needed help with his kid, and we weren't there to help. All I can think about is how much I want the Farmer to help me, to teach me, for his hands and his body to make me compliant.

I complain about butch things: I don't want to hike, or camp, or play basketball. All I want to do is hang out with the women in the kitchen, all I want to do is watch boys play with other boys. We lift weights one day, and he's spotting me, my head in front of his crotch, me lying down, him standing, dick dangling in plain grey sweats. He has a big dick. Later, he says: 'Every time you complain, but every time you have fun.'

What would have happened if I'd pulled down his pants when he was spotting me? What would have happened when, in that gym, a serious gym, with all those straight boys, all those hockey players and football jocks, all those thick oil-field workers and third-generation farmers trying to strip away decades of hard labour and replace it with an otter-sleek machine sheen? I imagine sucking him off, not in the locker room, not in the car back home, but in the middle of that gym, to his surprise, to the surprise of the other boys, to the surprise of other men. I imagine him slapping my hand away, violently dislodging it, and I also imagine him getting into it, thrusting hard and quick, tracing his member against the softness of my soft palate. I imagine him dropping the bar, and me almost choking against his warm prick, against the barbell.

The Farmer was supposed to protect my purity. He wanted me to be a good Mormon, and wanted me to be a good man, and he wanted me to make sure that I did the rituals that were required for that to happen. We went to the temple.

The temple was in Cardston, a collection of white marble rectangles, done by acolytes of Frank Lloyd Wright, on the crest of a hill, closer to the U.S. Border than the foothills. Cardston was a cattle town, and a cowboy town. The sugar beets in nearby Raymond were controlled, at least in part, by Mormon agribusiness, as was the corn in Taber, another nearby town. There weren't any bars in Raymond or Taber. Small towns in Alberta would have a bar downtown, with rooms above it, and if they were big enough, a Chinese restaurant attached. Cardston was big enough for a bar and a hotel, pious enough for a temple.

The founder of the town had four wives – he fled the States to protect them. He never touched a drop of liquor, and his letters were too discreet to discuss his desires, aside from wanting to better know about God. We didn't know who shared his bed, or how they shared his bed. The cowboys or shepherds would come in from the ranches on Saturday nights and sometimes they would dance; the other churches would have dances too, and sometimes they drank, and their Mormon neighbours didn't drink, so that was a bit of controversy, and sometimes they would go upstairs with a girl, and on Sunday that was scandal.

The Farmer and I drove down to Cardston after work on Sunday. I had passed a bishop's interview, and I was going to be the proxy for people who had died but communicated their desire to be baptized from beyond the grave.

There are a lot more Mormons in Southern Alberta, but there are Mormons throughout Alberta. We drove the five hours from Sherwood Park, down Highway 2, the church growing larger and larger before us. Mom's mom's family grew up west of that drive, and so we never quite visited them. If I think, I can remember the cities: Nisku (where the airport was); Leduc; Lacombe; Blackfalds; Red Deer, which I think of as halfway between Calgary and Edmonton, with Gasoline Alley and the giant teapot, and doughnuts that are still my favourite in all of Canada; Innisfail, where we would have to turn to see my mom's family, which was the difference between temple trips and trips home for Christmas and Easter; Crossfield, with the mural of the buck rider three storeys tall, the tallest public art north of Calgary and south of Edmonton; Airdrie; Calgary, seeping through the landscape now, like blood through sheets, like mud sludging and collapsing at the edge of a river – now everything from Airdrie to Calgary is one town.

We skirted Calgary, we missed Okotoks, we stopped to piss just before Nanton – natural springs, legendary sparkling water, I still remember an orange soda there, gorgeous and artifice-ridden, its own kind of blasphemy, as unnatural as any other desire I might have had. I looked for it later, but the internet has no memory. We stayed with the Farmer's in-laws. They took me to dinner at a Subway. I sat making small talk with this stranger about my faith, and I didn't know if I believed a word of it. I thought that I would do these actions, I would be baptized by proxy, and then I would be a better Mormon.

The baptisms took place inside a monumental limestone building settled on the crest of a hill.

The baptism was its own separation from this world and the world to come. The baptismal font was on the back of twelve oxen. The room resembled a Byzantine temple. The cathedral high space was interrupted only by a balcony thirty feet up, and above the balcony, Deco-style mosaics and frescoes of scenes from the Book of Mormon. A father put his hand on my back, he dropped me into the water, I rose; he did this again, and again, the monitor told of the names I was releasing: an insurance agent from the Midwest, a German prince. My sanctity and the baptizer's sanctity matched across this world and into the next. Even if I wasn't sanctified, the act was – what was the point of my own sanctity?

I have no idea who was there – maybe one or two of us. I remember sleeping quietly in a rumpus room. I was overtaken with lust, a lust that the church, the laying on of hands, the praying, and the hymn singing tried to alleviate. Still, all I wanted to do was fuck boys, all I wanted to do was join the women's relief society, all I wanted to do was be sealed forever for eternity, all I wanted to do was never go on a mission.

The body was abstracted into this material ritual, my body a tool for the Lord to use – but the Lord could only use bodies that he thought were men, and who were straight. I ended up neither of those things. I am formally not on the rolls of the church, formally no longer a member. Are the people for whom I was baptized in proxy still members? In leaving the church, did I rob them of their opportunities?

We wound our way through the darkening suburbs, settling for bed, saying bedtime prayers with these strangers, praying fervently. I couldn't sleep after everyone had gone to bed. I couldn't sleep and was anxious.

Half-hard, half considering options. There was a JCPenney catalogue from the mid-1990s, with the distinct possibility of a men's underwear section, and there was a large coffee table book of Michelangelo sculptures on the bookshelf, hidden amongst the hymn books and family home evening manuals. My fist pumping fast, searching for an image, my body working faster than my brain, belly down, on the wall-to-wall carpet, before anyone could discover me. I arrived and finished on a two-page spread of Michelangelo's sculpture *Dying Slave,* an overly muscled man taking his shirt off, his eyes rolling back in his head – masochism as ecstasy, a work that gave birth to half a millennium of queer aesthetics.

I splattered cum all over my belly and the carpet, on the edge of this coffee-table book, secret queer history, this figure groaning in ecstasy, stripped of shirt, with a bigger dick than classical heritage would suggest.

I would go to the temple in the morning. I must have cleaned up, but have no memory of being clean, or doing the cleaning. Just the shame of ersatz pornography. Another tradition, hidden from me, redeemed by accident, in that grand queer tradition of just enough.

# Lesson Six:
# Leaving Home;
# or, The Dorm Master Instills
# Discipline in a Strange Place

When I was twelve, my parents, under pressure from my grandmother and tired of my feralness, sent me away. The school was two hours from home. Edmonton is a string of small towns, feeder towns, sort-of suburbs, and actual suburbs; there was Fort Saskatchewan, my home, and Sherwood Park, where I went to church, and Edmonton, where we would go out every so often. And then the towns on the other side of the city, between Stony Plain and Spruce Grove, further to Wabamun Lake, the nearest small town, and the Genesee power plant, a bleak, grey building on the stone shore of an iron lake. Turn left, off the highway, to a gravel road, and right again, the crest of a hill on the banks of the North Saskatchewan River, a church, and a large school, recently rebuilt after arson.

The first meeting was with a teacher. Not even the headmaster, a dorm master. He would charm me, charm my parents. Let me into a side room, alone, for half an hour to fill out an intelligence exam – one that I had done before, in my history of psychologists and school counsellors, and eventually a severe psychiatrist I saw from age six to twelve. I don't think it was ever explained why I was there, what I was doing.

The school smelled of bleach and dirt and sweat, the windows half-drawn.

I saw boys working, making noise, playing outside, while I was concentrating on the test in front of me, bored, in some kind of reverie and some kind of terror, an erotic limbo that would last for the next two years. Draw a tree, make a house, tell a story, look up, see a boy without his shirt, answer general knowledge questions, make a pattern out of images provided. See a woman in a tight skirt, heels, blazer, she walks leaning back, slowly. Her whole body almost undulating, sidewinding from where she stays on campus, toward the school building, making the men, and some of the boys, pay attention. The man who greeted my mom and dad like he was my long-lost uncle came and put his hand hard on my shoulder, gathered the test, and took me into his office.

The Dorm Master told me that I needed discipline, that I was a bad kid, that I caused my parents heartbreak, that I didn't know how to be a man, and that he would make me a man. He told me my grandmother was nervous and my grandfather was rich, though no one ever told me about money. I found out later that making me a man was worth $30K a year, room and board, some weekends, all of June, some July, all of August free.

The bishop's interview: you would admit a sin, and the punishments were cosmic. They could be immediate, they could prevent you from being ordained, but it wasn't confession. You were never punished; it was just the disappointment of an ever-loving father – in Mormon cosmology, a father who had flesh and a body, but who was also God ('The Father has a body of flesh and bones as tangible as man's; the Son also' [D&C 130:22]). But here, the interview with the Dorm Master, a man who looked like a Daddy, and not a dad, a father and not a Daddy, again the dad/Daddy dialectic: he would tell of punishment, lines, time outs, or running miles, and these seemed suitable. Then he would send your parents out of the room, saying with great tenderness that he wanted to talk to you man-to-man, one-on-one. He would close the door; your parents would sit in an alcove beside the reception desk. The father would get up from his desk, he would sit beside you, in a chair, absent from your parents, as intimate as you have been with another man – not as intimate as you were with boys – and he would say, do you understand all of the rules, and he would take out a paddle. He talked about it as corporal punishment. And all punishment is bodily – though this is an understanding that would come to me decades later – emphasizing the body, reinforcing the body, breeding a new body, or the space where I become embodied.

Or it is a body that is not your own. The body is never yours. It lives in the community – some communities are more explicit than others. The body was the bishop's for a while, when he asked his questions; the body was God's when I was being baptized by proxy; and this time, with the Dorm Master, it felt like my body was given by my parents to this man, who seemed so eager to take it, to form it, to shape it. The bishop was the first person, it felt like, to understand that my hunger for looking was wanting, even at the age of twelve, to be its own kind of owning, to have my own kind of control of another's body. The Dorm Master's desire to control my body was his desire to move my boyhood into adulthood, his own desire to absorb his body into mine at the same time. Growing like a parasite.

He asked me if I wanted to test out the paddle. He asked me if I wanted to bend over the desk. He said spankings were rare, but if I were curious, I could have a taste.

It was universally acknowledged that my dad was a fuck-up, unable to parent, unable to be a father. In that good Freudian way, I sought endless replacements who could teach me all sorts of things. The Dorm Master was one of those; the bishop was another. The Dorm Master was not the bishop, but the dad/Daddy in one figure, the dad/Daddy a monster who knew how to tenderly grow a boy. A Daddy who would end up failing at that eventual wish.

# Lesson Seven:
# Are Boys Who Took Care
# of Me Daddies?

## The Scion

On the boarding school's annual hike, Grade 12 students would take care of the new boys in Grade 7. There was a loop: the old boys would teach the new boys, which would suggest that it was their last act, the last big trip – the Drayton Valley trip, their last as students at the school. The staff would teach the basics: how to pack a backpack, how to tie shoes properly, how to keep things dry and safe, how to avoid being eaten by bears. The old boys would also teach more complicated skills: how to determine hierarchies, how to make sure that you were never on the bottom, how to mainstream, how to mock, how to be a boy, how to avoid being eaten by each other. They would show their dominance in ways that seemed unusually cruel.

I was raped at that school. But it was part of a matrix of other behaviours. Up until the late nineties, we were still paddled. I was paddled thirty-two times in Grade 7. Each time was between one and seven swats. Most of the paddling was done by a teacher, who would occasionally end the sessions by touching my penis. The touching was pleasure, the swatting was violence, and it took me more than two decades of various therapists and a court case to recognize that, at twelve years old, no matter what I wanted, I was coerced; that what I wanted, and what was right for him to give, were radically different.

I decided before going to this school to become vegetarian, and I went through my first four days there without eating meat. One night near the end of the eight-day hike, I had to eat meat, and, afraid that I would throw it up, I went into the woods, away from the campsite. The old boys followed me into the woods to supervise, and to piss with me. This solved more than the vegetarian problem. In the marking of territory, in making straight boys, in playing chicken with how close you can be before being a faggot, to mark themselves as wild – even against civilization – straight boys piss together. (I learned how to stand up in a canoe to piss. The canoes there held ten people. The other nine applauded.)

One of the boys who followed me was the son of a prominent rancher from Mormon country, though he wasn't Mormon. And I don't think he even spoke along when we said Compline, an Anglican prayer before sleep.

The boarding school was Anglican. We had a mid-week mass, and evening prayers once a week. When we went out into the wilderness, hiking or canoeing, the evening prayer would occur daily, in the small time after dinner and before lights out. Mormonism's litany is very often spontaneous, and the bits that aren't are plain and American. The re-enacting of this archaic English, by young boys who barely spoke their own language, is its own kind of framing: rites of safety in the middle of danger – the primal danger of the woods, and the perhaps more primal danger of other human beings.

Compline contained the lines *Save us, Lord, while we are awake; protect us while we sleep; that we may keep watch with*

*Christ and rest with him in peace.* It ends with the words *The Lord grant us a quiet night and a perfect end.*

*Night* here being both literal and metaphorical. *End* being the end of the day and end of life. We were reminded of our own death. After Compline, I would go to the bathroom one more time, and the Scion would walk me into the woods, to supervise, because the staff were worried that I would puke out my dinner.

He pulled his cock out of his khakis. It was thick, uncut – and I looked at it, had never seen anyone else's, never looked over in the washroom, except in the locker room for the odd swimming lesson. He asked if I was piss shy, he mocked my being piss shy, and so I pushed my cock out of my pants and started to piss. He finished and started tugging on his foreskin. I looked and he looked, and he kept tugging, and I didn't know what to do next. His rough hand grabbed my cock, I wrenched back; he mocked me, suggested that I was naive. He kept jacking off in front of me. It was obvious that I was hard. He finished, I watched. The next day after Compline, we were back in the woods. There, he pushed my head down; he shoved his cock through my clenched teeth. Kneeling on the soft forest floor, moss and pine. It tasted sour, like sweat and stale piss. We went back, and I went to bed. On the third day, he had gotten what he wanted twice, and he went further than I thought possible. He dragged me deeper into the woods. The first time, we could see the camp; there was plausible deniability. The second time, we could hear the camp, and he was risking being caught – why did you go so far out, what are you doing in the darkness of the woods?

The third time, we could not see or hear the camp. We went through the woods; we went past a stream – like convicts trying to escape bloodhounds. He pushed me down then, he pulled me up, he hit me. He stripped me. He was hard, I was no longer hard, he pushed his prick through my asshole. It hurt, it burnt and felt like I was being pulled apart from the inside. He yanked my hair. It must have lasted five minutes.

Those five minutes expanded my mind, opened me to other possibilities, gave me thoughts about power and desire, made me learn to love what I should hate. The Mormons believe that in the 1830s, in Upstate New York, a boy wandered into the woods, got down on his knees, prayed, and God came as three separate beings. When I was a boy, I was marched into the woods, forced down on my knees, and was opened to a new world – one marked by violence, and a fear of those difficult landscapes, especially when the exterior landscape rotted into the interior one.

## The River Rat

He was in Grade 8 when I was in Grade 7. Sweet, kind, generically handsome. He had a body that was on the right side of built. The River Rat and I went to the woods together during exam seasons, when he got out early and I got out early. He discovered me in the dorm, asked if I wanted to go for a walk, and I thought either he liked me or he was slumming, and I was willing to be slummed with. The school fundraised by bottling and selling our own honey, so the road behind the steel outbuilding where we did this was called Honey Hill – the smell of thousands of litres of honey has a musk that smells like boys sweating together. He had a backpack, and we never had backpacks around the school; we also rarely took walks. There was a run once a week where you got a mile per demerit, and there were six snowshoe runs between November and February, plus practice runs, and portage practices in the fall, plus whatever rugger (a less elegant, more primitive riff on rugby), hockey, and football games we managed to fit in. Unplanned walks were unusual. (Wilderness must be mapped; to be off the map is to be in danger – the snowshoe runs, in ever larger loops around the property, went occasionally into riverbanks and creek beds, but always mapped, never wilderness.) To be with the River Rat, to have this walk, to not know what was in the backpack, to be in this idyllic space with an older boy, that sweet space after the end of the last exam and before the river runs: the interior wilderness made up for the lack of exterior wilderness.

We went behind the honey house – we went down the gravel road, we crossed the potato field diagonally. We walked to the edge of the poplar bluffs, down the sandstone cliffs, to the edge of the river – a river still wet with spring mud. There was small talk, the same small talk that was awkward and that I have failed at ever since – about teachers, classes, and the exams I just took. It's been two decades; can I remember a conversation that occurred two decades ago?

Think of this as allegory, think of this as how to write biography, think of this as a composite profile, think of this as fiction, think of this as only as real as you need it to be.

What was in the backpack? A blanket, a Discman, a copy of a Nirvana album, half a pack of smokes, a can of Pil, a seventies-era *Hustler* or something harder than *Playboy*. The next year, an entire grey market of underground porn was discovered by a teacher who paraded it through the dorms. There was a cheap science-fiction paperback, a bag of chips – everything that we were not supposed to have.

It was like Whitman, or I think about it like Whitman, but every time I return to *Leaves of Grass*, I forget how Whitman's bodies were everyone's, swimming, and that his poems about swimming were about twenty-eight boys, and though there were times when we all went down and swam in that river, the River Rat and I never swam in that space. Maybe it's like Whitman because when I was in Grade 9, a friend from the school bought me a copy of *Leaves of Grass* because we had been reading Ginsberg, and what pretentious boys do after reading Ginsberg is give each other copies of Whitman.

It's also sort of like A. E. Housman because we were Anglican, and boys getting together on the riverbank in an Anglican context always brings up Housman:

> Far in a western brookland
> That bred me long ago
> The poplars stand and tremble
> By pools I used to know.
>
> There, in the windless night-time,
> The wanderer, marvelling why,
> Halts on the bridge to hearken
> How soft the poplars sigh.

So, this is context, and this might be a jangle or a tangent, or a dogleg – what did we do by the river?

The North Saskatchewan, thick with brown silt that spring from melted pack ice and mountain runoffs, runoffs that made the current visible, on the edge of the cliffs, pines and spruce, the scrabble of roots and broken branches built up to the end of that cliff – we sit on the branches, or we sit at the edge of the sandstone, looking at the sand crumbling, exposing roots – again another awkward metaphor, treat this as the obligatory Canadian Wilderness excerpt.

We drank a beer; we smoked two darts (they were better than the Drayton Valley canoe trip smokes). We listened to some Nirvana. Eventually the sun warmed us enough, and we took our shirts off. We looked at porn. We talked about girls. We bragged about things that never happened. We didn't talk about what was happening in school. We dared each other to go further. He read a chapter of whatever novel he was working on. We watched the river move. I thought about his dick. I thought about my dick. We got hard, and we got a little buzzed, and we thought about swimming. We realized it was twenty minutes before dinner.

On the canoe trip later that year, I had his dick in my hand: thicker than I thought it would be, curved toward his belly. On the edge of the South Saskatchewan, and so for completeness, for a good Albertan parenthesis, I want to think that we did something that day.

I don't remember. The narrative frustrates me.

But, for all the songs and stories about what happens near the riverbank, or on the river – about girls and kissing – I can only think of how Kip Moore sings, in 'Somethin' 'Bout a Truck,' about the kind of attraction that happens between two people at 2 a.m., with not a lot of clothes, some beer, and a lot of time before the sun comes up. There was something about a river, around 4 p.m., after two of those beers, etc. But we were never naked, and we never kissed. Jerking off next to each other, jerking each other off – well, that's just what happens when boys get together. It's an accident, it's the isolation of the West, it's the place where homosociality can be an excuse. Plausible deniability. I wonder if that's why the River Rat and I never swam, though we were on the bank. I know that's what boys who like girls get: first kisses. And boys who like boys get to sentimentalize hand jobs.

Canoeing Drayton Valley, that wide, slow curve of a river, those sandbar islets in the middle of Canada's Mississippi: first drink of whisky, first beer, first smoke, first weed, cocks in my hand, and cocks on display – an island of lost boys. The adults would leave us alone on that trip, and for a weekend, the Grade 12 boys were in charge – the freedom of that environment, control and then release, control and then release, with some plausible deniability besides. The Grade 12 boys, some being legal adults, would smuggle all the contraband. Though there were supposed to be bag checks, none of them were ever done on that one trip.

The trip was done between the end of the school year and the longer canoe trips. Those were the idylls of vice, a small respite between the overpacked school year and the toxic pressure of canoeing sixty kilometres or more a day. That weekend, we drank Pilsner, which went from the local shitty beer of my childhood, a dad beer like O'Keefe Extra Old Stock, to cooler than PBR when I was ageing out of the Montreal hipster scene. We smoked Peter Jacksons, a discount brand, only slightly cheaper than Rez smokes, but also because the headmaster shared its name, and bored rich kids have an expert ironist aesthetic. To smoke, to drink, to roughhouse, to spit, and to piss, those were things the bodies could do that would mark them as boys and would give them permission to be men. Even in tales of being forced to suck someone off, or forcing someone to eat a biscuit after a dozen boys had cum on it, the lack of consent marked a kind of masculine effort. There was a subtext that you could bully, and perhaps rape, someone into masculinity.

To want to rest a hand on someone's back, to rest a head on a lap, to sit in the half dark on a warm spring day and read next to someone, and the acts that occurred in private, in tents and off the side of campgrounds, coded to be masc … The River Rat's kindness occurred only outside of these packs, and I never got as much as I wanted from him, but I got more from him than some boys, and less from him than others.

## The Ploughboy

At 6'6", 240 lbs., the Ploughboy was built by hauling hay on his family's farm in Central Alberta. He moved, talked, and smoked and ran and played rugger like a train; when he slowed down to something less recreational, he loped, back swayed, shoulders straight. The Ploughboy had blue eyes and a spit curl that accentuated those eyes. He wore too-tight Wranglers and too-tight T-shirts, the kind of T-shirts you would buy in packs of three at SAAN's. He had a perpetual five-o'clock shadow, and hair peeking out of his sleeves and collar. I never saw the Ploughboy take his shirt off, never saw him on canoe trips, never saw him anywhere but study hall. He didn't supervise me on chores, didn't lead my canoe trips, didn't work in the kitchen. I was never sure of what he did or who he was. All I knew is that when I saw him in chow line or walking to study hall, he was taller and more confident than any person in the room, and I knew that he would get into a lot of good trouble.

I was in the lounge one day, killing time and reading. There must have been half a dozen people there, and there was that kind of silly chat people that age get into. Someone asked him how it was hanging, and he described his cock: the length and girth of it, the state of its circumcision, where it rested against his thigh, how prodigious his loads were. It was stated in that long, low-key monotone, like he was describing what he ate for dinner. Someone described it – in earshot, though I was eavesdropping – that the Ploughboy was young, dumb, and full of cum. Thinking about him later – sweaty, stinking, hair matted against chest and under his arms – imagining that cock, it's all I wanted to do: to taste his cock full of piss, to slather my mouth all over it and after that to have the sweat and the cum and the piss commingle with my own sweat and slobber.

I know when boys talk about their cocks they exaggerate. I still think that the Ploughboy was telling the truth – just how confident he was in a place that worked to make sure everyone was anxious.

I still am not sure I want a cock; I don't like my cock – too unreliable, ugly, and tender – too like an orchid. I want to replace it with something – not with a cunt, but there is a reason I prefer the polymorphous perversity, the multi-use function of tongues and fingers. Almost all the boys who were sure of their cocks I knew were not safe, not present. The Ploughboy was the only man whose surety marked a kind of commitment to place.

That moment in the lounge will collapse into memory, and that memory will stretch into other spaces. The question of whether I want a specific body part for my own enjoyment or if I want someone to impose their own body on my body, if I want that imposition to last a minute, a month, or a life, is still ambivalent.

I don't think that the Ploughboy ever thought about his cock for more than a minute – he was that kind of straight boy whose cock always worked, and who he was and who he wanted matched with an elegant sameness, a one-to-one correlation. Looking at the Ploughboy, thinking of his cock entering me, wanting for a moment to have that entering be its own kind of anointing, a kind of high transfer magic – your perfect penis, in my imperfect mind, will make my body behave, will refuse the ambivalence of my gender, will make my boyhood firm. Even now, thinking of the Ploughboy I retreat from his 'born this way' essentialism and move on to a post-queer, post-gender Bartleby – I would prefer not to, not to be a boy, not to be respectable, not to be sweet and delightsome, not to be beholden to what is assumed is my biology.

The Ploughboy is the only man whose surety marked a kind of commitment to plainness.

## The Game Master

I remember, on a winter camping trip, this boy confessed that he had played with another boy, in a quiet and discreet way (played with the other boy in a discreet way, told me in a discreet way). He was the first person I asked to touch me – or for me to touch him, for something consensual, uncomplicated, explicit, and mutual. He refused in an incredulous tone. I mentioned this in a fight once – in front of another kid, and he volleyed back: me getting in shit for wanting, getting in shit for asking.

Later, on a canoe trip, I got a little bit of what I wanted. On the hikes, on snowshoe trips, on canoe trips, we would pretend to play Dungeons and Dragons, no dice, no rules, nothing but stories. Stories of the most classic 'someone leaves town, someone comes to town' archetype. I do not know if we even chose characters. Some of us had played a little before school, but the informality of the thinking seemed key to the enterprise. I don't think we played formal D&D in the school. I don't think anyone had dice.

On this canoe trip, we played D&D with two other kids. It must have been a rest day, or recreation time in the late afternoon. The talk got dirtier and dirtier, subtly, and then collapsed into filth. A story about four bards and a tavern. Game Master was telling the story, and he introduced this magical pocket pussy, which would fold itself over any cock. As he talked, he started rubbing his hand over his pants, and the other boy began doing something similar. He added more details, about sizes and shapes of this magical pussy, about all the artificial things this magic pussy could do – the sort of details that I assume didn't come from any real experience.

Eventually, the first boy took his cock out of his pants, that half-clipped cock, with a bulging frenulum, his foreskin retreated, his glans engaged, and, in that, emerged permission for the two of us. I think there was explicit permission-seeking too – something sweet and awkward on my behalf, something about wanting to be good or not offending, or not noticing. Even in the midst of this conversation about pocket pussies, even in this narrative intending to get us off, even with the other boys with their cocks, half or fully out of their flies, I had to ask, *Can I take my cock out, can I play?*

Being on a canoe trip was an attempt to use the wilderness to mould young minds, an idea of the wilderness, another crafting of Arcadia. Having the boys tell a story of sex in the middle of the woods was creating another kind of paradise, against the creation of parents and teachers. This story was an imaginary city, an act of resistance. An anti-Arcadia. An argument for sex.

There was no touching, no circle jerking, just storytelling and cock playing for an audience. An act that has occurred since Chaucer, and an act that would centre what I liked for decades in the future. Tell me a dirty story, show me your inner bits, text and body intermingling.

I remember, afterward, when the first boy and I shared a tent, one of the teachers said that we fought like a married couple. Thinking of the dozen times on the trip that Game Master and I watched each other masturbate, I was going to say, 'And we fuck like one too.' But what does a married couple fuck like, and what would I even know about that back then?

# Lesson Eight:
# Arcadia Burns

Three weeks after the new-boy hike, I was pulled aside by the Dorm Master, who told me that I had to behave better, to be better, to be cleaner, and neater, and more precise.

Twenty-six years after this, the Dorm Master went to trial for what I am about to describe. The trial was in a small-town multi-purpose centre on a jury-rigged stage. The questions from the Dorm Master's defence lawyer were about the exact location of rooms in the school – there were blueprints and builders' reports. The assumption was that the private act of spanking was public enough to mean that the more private, more sexual acts would also be public. The sound would leak.

The Dorm Master told me that, from that point on, he would make sure I took two showers a day. He would supervise the showers himself. He would do this ordinarily, often peeping his head in, often watching – but this watching would be formal.

The shower had a vestibule, and then the room itself. Six boys, three on each side. There were no dividers, no curtain – a small square and a large square – the shape, the inner and the outer, oddly reminded me of the shape of the tabernacle. Every shower was a competition, a gang of bodies and pretending not to gaze.

The Dorm Master, the man who interviewed me, who showed me the paddle, spanked me thirty-two times in the nine months that he knew me. After every third spank, he would touch my penis. Toward the end of the year, he asked me to touch his. Just before the end of the year, he walked me to the woods, and he pulled his penis out of his trousers. Pretending to piss or maybe pissing, a reasonable excuse, a plan, something more – but I put my mouth on the lips of his cock.

In legal contexts, there is a semantic difference between *in* and *on* with regards to the penis and the lips. So, officially, now according to the State, we agree about the touching, and that something else occurred, but disagree about what that something else might be.

All I remember is wanting his cock in my mouth. I like a cock in my mouth, hardening and fulling, warm and stiff like pudding rising, like quick-set cement, like velvet cast in iron.

The lawyers were very concerned about the surface versus the interior of the mouth. They asked if I could remember whether I opened my mouth, whether he opened my mouth, whether my mouth was opened at all. I remember the roughness of the Scion, the shove and the collapse and the entering like a battering ram against the softness; and I remember the gentility of the Dorm Master, and giving everything that I could want to him, and I imagine, at that moment, it was an *in* and not an *on*.

At twelve, what do you want? At twelve, you beg to stay up late because you cannot imagine morning, at twelve you want to eat nothing but candy for dinner, at twelve you have nothing good in your heart. I doubt that I could say no to the Dorm Master, but I remember jerking off to him in the first weeks of school, and I remember his touch after the spanking. The cold, methodical, percussive hit of paddle on flesh, and then the softness. The Dorm Master wasn't a blue-collar working man, no calluses, no roughness – the tenderness of hand-on-hand, the tenderness of flesh-on-flesh.

A twelve-year-old cannot go up to a forty-year-old and say: 'I want your hand on my cock.' A forty-year-old cannot say: 'I want to touch a twelve-year-old's cock.' Desire shall not be said out loud. There was a woman in the school who all the boys would lust after. The lust was a feedback loop. There were rumours about other female staff – about appearances in *Playboy*, and about violence – a sense of ownership over their bodies, mirrors on shoes to look up skirts, accidental-on-purpose touching.

The boys would talk about the English teacher, the math teacher, or the headmaster's wife, about how much they wanted to fuck these women. They would talk morning, noon, and night about how they imagined these women. They would tell stories, and the stories would have endless details. The oldest stories, repeating and building, abstractions built on real flesh.

Those boys never got to fuck the women they wanted to fuck. There were men and women in that school, teachers that I wanted to fuck – the math teacher who looked like Neal Cassady, the aforementioned English teacher, the wife of the headmaster, the man who ran my snowshoe run – and boys I wanted to fuck, and some of those boys I did, and none of the adults I did, except for the Dorm Master. *Fuck* widely defined.

I was so in awe of the aura of power that the Dorm Master allowed that I have no memory of his cock, though I have more of a memory of his hands and the potential of his mouth. The gap between the bodies and landscapes – this imaginary of land, this invention of wilderness, of the woods, is key here, again and again.

On the new-boy hike, in order to fuck my mouth and my ass, the Scion walked away from camp, into the woods. The Dorm Master initiated oral contact in the woods. The woods were more like the classical Arcadia, a space where everything is brought into a calmed harmony, where nature and humanity function as one, a space that ignores danger. A space has to be dangerous enough for the transformative risk to occur – for the punishment to be seen as real – but it has to be crafted and artificial enough that the ambivalence about what is real and what is artificial leads to a profound instability. And you have to sell the transcendence of nature to anxious adults who are spending in the mid-five figures for their kids to be there. Wilderness is nature codified – the codifying of the internal and the external.

One of the goals of this school was to tame boys, to bring them into the wilderness to learn how to be men. One of the goals of the spanking is a similar taming, and this double taming mirrors the public/private of the duty master's room. The duty master is a role that exists when one is looking after children for a certain period of time; dorm master is the adult or teacher in charge of a class explicitly. A dorm master can be a duty master, but so can every other adult male.

The Scion, when he was acting as duty master, would risk acts (the cock in the mouth, the cock up the ass) because the wilderness is supposed to be untamed, but also because the ambivalence of that space allowed for a new kind of pedagogy. The sex at the school was about anything but the actual cock in the actual mouth, the cock in the actual hand, then the rupture in the body is saying out loud that the cock and the hand and the cock and the mouth and the cock and the asshole were an act of base faggotry – that coming with the Dorm Master was a step out of the closet, was a wish fulfilled, that meeting with the Dorm Master again was a desire to return back to an Arcadian space, where one could be one of Whitman's boys:

> Little streams pass'd all over their bodies.

> An unseen hand also pass'd over their bodies,
> It descended tremblingly from their temples and ribs.

> The young men float on their backs, their white bellies
>     bulge to the sun, they do not ask who seizes fast to
>     them …

I gave evidence two years before the trial, sometimes in Hamilton and sometimes in small-town Alberta – to cops who were mostly indifferent (though one was a perfect small-town cop as if cast by Bob Mizer). One could not retreat at that moment – the cop led to the Crown Prosecutor, who didn't work for you but for the State. The Crown suggested I hire my own lawyer. He said that they would not arrest me if I didn't go, but that I was legally obligated (to fly in the middle of a pandemic, at the tail end of winter, to get in a cab to be driven to the edge of yet another prairie city, to stay at a Best Western). The Crown Prosecutor, and my friends who came to support me, and another small-town cop and the security guards all met in this tiny storage room of that community centre. Most of my first day of testimony was arguments and cajoling about pronouns and memory. I could have a nice job in a city far away from here, I could change my names, I could go by they or them or

Mx, I could fuck dozens of people in a dozen cities in three countries, and these boys of the State would conspire to get me into that small room and tell their stories – that I was lying about the Dorm Master, or that what the Dorm Master did to me was unforgivably vile.

The Arcadia burned to the ground, like the rest of the Western grasslands, that summer.

The philosopher Guy Hocquenghem had sex with his teacher when he was fifteen. That teacher's name was René Schérer. Soon after the protests and strikes of May '68 in Paris, they wrote a book about the experience, which was published in 1976. It was an act of making the private public. It was an explicit act of scandal and using scandal as a tool of self-liberation. It is an impossible book to read now – very much of its time and very much a book of Schérer trying to convince Hocquenghem of the theoretical basis of acts that are now profoundly taboo. It is an act of pedagogy and of liberation of children. Reading a samizdat translation, I wonder if 'intellectually defending' instead of resting on praxis, if pretending that a man having sex with a child is a political act, is worse or better than the simple praxis of hand on cock … I don't know. Hearing someone being spanked makes a private act a public body. Having a hand on a cock is a private body – it is our secret; we will not tell anyone. The direct, visceral pleasure retreats into abstraction. Allowing that moment to be an act of queer desire, an initiating act of identity – alone in that room, that moment, even without discussion – allowing the estranging of pleasure into a nascent identity abstracts the directness of body-to-body contact.

The spanking is the public body, the *corps* of *esprit de corps* and the heterosexualization of homosocial humiliation, as found in prisons and reform camps and the rest. The private subject is what happens after – but it is not private because the Dorm Master is trying to recruit. He is the homophobic monster that the bourgeois-ization of same-gender desire pretends does not exist. The queer theorist Eve Kosofsky Sedgwick talks about this in her essay 'A Poem Is Being Written':

> I know we were always spanked, in a careful orchestration of spontaneity and pageantry, 'simply' over the parental lap, the spanking in my imagination (I can only barely stop myself from saying, the spanking that is my imagination) has always occurred over a table, a table scaled precisely to the trunk of the child, framing it with a closeness and immobilizing exactitude that defined, for me, both the English word truncate and the French, of course, tableau.

I made a mistake. The Dorm Master brings me to the duty master's room. He bends me over a bed. A piece of one-by-two, carved in the wood shop, is stored in the room. He swats me. He tells me what I have done wrong.

The Dorm Master's lawyer asks about pageantry, I am asked about this pageantry. We disagree about the paperwork, but we agree about the act of spanking itself. The bed is as domestic as Sedgwick's table. The Dorm Master pretended to be our father, and the Dorm Master made the landscape that he inhabited domestic. The trial's questions are about the physical spaces that the Dorm Master occupied: the room he stayed in, the showers where he watched boys, the dining room, and the study halls.

I went from the boarding school, in Grades 7 and 8, to a locked ward in the hospital, and so the question of where I felt most at home was always open.

To do wrong is to beg to be hit, to beg to be hit is to desire to be touched in lower and grosser forms.

# Lesson Nine:
# The Clinic

How do you return to freedom after the strong regimentation of a reform school? How do you walk home and live in your own bedroom when you have spent the last two years in a dormitory? How do you fill the hours between four and seven, between after school and when Mom comes home, when for the past two years you had that schedule tightly contained? How do you become a child again – when, for the previous two years, you were systematically told that you were not a child? It's hard to be a kid when you have done all the things that adults are supposed to do: lived away from home, learned how power works, had a day job and a *job* job, drank, and smoked, and had cocks in hands or mouth. How do you become an adult, even at fourteen, when you are convinced that your parents didn't like or trust you enough that you had to go away? Especially when the system intends to isolate, to quash and destroy any attempts at solidarity.

So, you sort of don't go to classes. You scream. You stay up past midnight. You develop a light shoplifting habit. You go feral on your classmates: filthy, untamed, angry, and provocative. All upset tables and upset people. I don't remember my behaviour; I don't remember the chaos of it. I don't remember anyone asking what happened when I went away from school, but it was decided that the best strategy was to go away to school again.

I spent my Grade 9 year as an in-patient at an adolescent psychiatric facility.

The first time I was there, and for three months after, there was a behaviour contract, and we would negotiate what I could or couldn't do, and if I was a good boy (always boy – I wonder if for most of my childhood the emphasis was less on *good* and more on *boy*, a boy could only be good if they were a boy).

Good boys didn't smoke, they didn't fuck, they didn't drink, they didn't talk back, they bussed their tables, they ate what was given to them, they wore hula hoops on their hips so they could know where their body began and the other body stopped, they played floor hockey from 4 p.m. to 5 p.m., they made their beds, they shaved their faces, they brushed their hair and their teeth, they went on Accutane and risperidone, and all the other ways of making their bodies and their minds complement each other. They were boys.

There was less sex in the ward, more chances to be caught, more willingness to punish those who were less discreet.

Two people to a room in the hospital, thus two ways of setting up those beds. The first set-up was two beds parallel to each other, facing a desk, with the bathroom on the left, closest to the door. There was a small closet across from the bathroom, and a table between the two beds. There were headboards that you could stack things on, and there were drawers underneath the beds. The other set-up had the second bed perpendicular against the far wall, its head at the window, its feet at the door. That second type of bedroom had a bathroom tucked in the far corner. The window in the bathroom was obscured with a thin sheet of milk-white opaque acrylic. The ward had been built in the 1960s or 1970s, and so it was all aqua and seafoam, none of the obsequious pastel corals of the 1990s, none of the odd mustards of the 1950s.

There is a conceptual artist, born in Hamilton, now living in Paris, named Kapwani Kiwanga, and she had a show a few years ago at the Esker Foundation Contemporary Art Gallery in Calgary called *A wall is just a wall (and nothing more at all)*. One part of that show was a series of paintings on drywall. They were an anthology of the social history of colour and hospitals – aesthetics as a kind of curing – with two colours on these large sheets, one on top and one on the bottom, looking like colour-field paintings from the 1970s, which had a century of pseudoscience behind them. Looking through them, I saw anxiety – this was the green of the locked ward's bathroom; this was the pink of my year doing suicide watch as a security guard at another hospital; this was the green of the university hospital; this was the sickly yellow of the wards when my mom was out of the ICU; this was the accent burgundy of the hospital from the last time I was hospitalized for trying to kill myself. This was the aqua of the hospital bathroom where one of my roommates mounted me.

Vulpine and sleek, evasive about why he was in the facility, about his family, about where he lived and where he was going back to, the Roommate was quiet, and his quietness was all-consuming. I don't remember the first time that he articulated wanting something sexual from me. I remember sleeping with him maybe a handful of times. I remember him telling me that he wanted to masturbate, announcing it, in the middle of the night – no privacy, under constant surveillance. I wasn't sure if it was a warning or an invitation.

The lessons that are taught directly reverse themselves, they point to potentials that one might not have imagined. Being told to stay home means that outside of home is even more seductive; being told that the only path forward is domestic makes one realize that the pleasures that exist in cities – outside of real estate, outside of children – are possible. Every no is a widening, wondering yes. The problem with options then becomes a question of how to find them, where to find them – and, by extension, how to systemize those discoveries.

In the dark, the Roommate and I would jerk off at the same time, maybe two or three times in a row. Listening carefully to the bed checks the overnight staff would do to make sure we were sleeping, to the other kids, and eventually, when we knew that we were alone, to our own rhythms – my slowing down to his speeding up, my speeding up to his slowing down, following patterns of skin-on-skin, noise of skin-on-skin, hoping to cum at the same time. There are stories of frat boys, in my pornographic readings, who would be so plain with their bodies that they would kid or joke, throw lotion to each other, race each other – none of this here. He didn't even announce it after that one time. I remember waiting for the bed check to end, waiting for the snap of an elastic waistband, waiting for a hand against thin cotton, and starting when he started, the soft mewl when finishing.

A few weeks later, the Roommate would show me, and he and I would sit next to each other; at first, no touching, just watching. Then him guiding my hand to his cock, and then his flat hand on mine as an introduction, then him curving his hand against the length of my cock – like how you let a dog lick the flat palm of your hand before you pet it, like the distance between a slap and a punch, like the power of an open hand and the hostility of a closed fist, light and slow and hard and fast – the mutuality becoming something like power.

Then he asked if he could enter me; he didn't say *fuck me*, he didn't say *cock in my ass*, he didn't say *screw*, but he also didn't say *enter* – I don't remember the vocabulary of how a working-class kid from the North would ask to split someone's asshole open with his cock. He was tall and scrawny, long cock, not thick but long, curved toward his belly. I remember at least twice he and I lay on the floor between the two beds (in order not to be discovered?), pants to our knees, him putting his whole body over me, his cock between my thighs, and then his hot breath in my ear, breathing deep, and I breathed, and he slipped in – the short, shock-sharp pain and he was in, the asshole engulfs the cock. It's not a penetration, but an argument between bodies, between the propulsive one and the engulfing one, between the active and the passive, a pas de deux of barely present consent.

I had to pretend that I had never done this before. The Roommate liked to pretend that he was teaching me something new. Sometimes he talked about all the things that he was teaching me, so that I would eventually learn how to please a girl; a few times the *girl* became a more permanent *girlfriend*; once, the *girlfriend* became *a wife*. I doubt he thought he was preparing me for heterosexual church; I was only ever passive for him, and though we never talked about this, I wonder if he thought this passivity was another way of being a girl.

I waited for him to ask, and he didn't ask often. Getting ready for a Christmas party, one of the fancy ones, funded by the police benevolent fund and featuring a central casting, local news bottle blonde singing 'Santa Baby' in too-tight, white faux-fur-trimmed crimson satin. Forced to play nice, stressed, and exhausted, we were grooming ourselves in that aqua bathroom when he reached behind me to get something from the sink and pressed his whole body against me, half-hard. I pushed back. We were arguing about something dumb, about who was smarter or had money, or some other kind of insecurity, and all of that dropped. We pulled my dress pants down (polyester, BiWay or Sears, black church pants), and he took his dripping member – I braced myself against the white porcelain – and instead of entering me, knowing he had ten or fifteen minutes, pushed against my thighs. I closed my thighs against his. Oscar Wilde's favourite position. The Roommate, like one of those Wildean barrow boys (Wilde thought he was saving poor kids from themselves; the hospital thought they were saving me). He thought he was teaching me, but he was also in favour of his own pleasure. When Wilde exchanged money for sex with working-class boys, there was a transparency there – a few quid for a few minutes – and when Wilde pretended that he was teaching the boys a special kind of civilization, he was lying to himself and lying to the boys. When he got mixed up with Bosie, the self-loathing bisexual and noted anti-Semite, when the act became a trading of texts, of mutually reinforcing pretension, he got into trouble. Wilde had all kinds of language and ritual to get what he wanted. The Roommate didn't. He wanted his cock between my thighs, he wanted things slick and slippery, wanted my own discomfort in the midst of a kind of public performance where everyone was playing nice. That seemed more accurate than his claim that I would outgrow these acts, that these were rehearsals for adult life.

The thighs would do the role of what the ass would do. Efficient, but not less erotic for their readiness. It was the decadent sex I would want as an adult, the sex I would later read about in Updike novels, sex that had the hint of ennui and the kind of historical distance you would see in Ang Lee's *The Ice Storm.* For a kid who wanted to be nothing but sophisticated, a little tryst in the bathroom before a party, ass and thighs red and damp from cum and sweat, sitting, stewing while the cops give you bad gifts and a kids' choir sings about Jesus – never more decadent than you were at fourteen.

# Dance Break

A church dance was where I discovered my queerness widening. I was convinced at that point, from all the evidence, that I was gay. I remember a church dance, lights low, a heavily curated playlist. I remember slow dancing with a girl, in retro, vintage, polyester taffeta (no one did mid-nineties thrift-store slacker ironic dress better than young Mormons – the exquisite push against firm dress codes). The girls were so kind, and they were so patient (like that first boy was, when he lifted my kid's body onto his near-adult shoulders). My hand on the hip, my hand on the shoulder, bodies close enough to get ideas but far enough not to fall into sin – enough room for the holy spirit, enough room for a Book of Mormon between us. The boys didn't dance with boys, except in groups, and the girls sometimes danced with girls, but never so close. So, I had my hands on this girl, was awkwardly but enthusiastically leading or being led across the dance floor, and as we were swaying, my eyes would drift over to her brother, the chaperone, returned from his mission, in that cheap navy suit and back to the girl, back and forth, and this must have happened a dozen times.

The church dances came with a little card; the card had the written rules on one side, and a schedule of dances on the other. The rules were simple things – that we had to wear dress pants, a tie, and a button-up shirt, that we had to dance far enough apart that there was no proof of temptation, that we could not dance in ways that upset God. There were no prohibitions about same-sex dancing, about drinking or smoking, about drug use – because it was beyond the pale. The dances provided a small good time on the weekends, a distraction, a bower from the world, and a way to sublimate bodily desires.

I knew that I was not going on a mission, so I didn't have the desire to fill up on earthly pleasures before becoming monastic for a few years. I knew that I had experienced a number of vices that no one else in this room had, and so my desire was not to remain in an arcadia but to return back to an arcadia.

The church dances were supposed to be a way to get married eventually, to distract until someone went off on a mission. All the single people in the room together, work and joy, in that church cultural hall, with the basketball guides woven into the plain grey carpet. When that girl swept me across the floor, sometimes I wanted to sleep with her, sometimes my body reacted with sweat or shortness of breath, or every so often the start of a hardening cock. When I looked over her shoulder, with a pleasant kind of cotton-headed sense – the closest I got to being tipsy in those sober spaces – my dancing partner and I were one, and the boy waiting for the next dance was one, and the brother taking care of his sister was one with me, and the other girls dancing next to me, plus the other dancing with him. We were all one body – a body politic, a body of Christ, a body of tradition, a body without self. So, when I say that I discovered queerness at those Mormon church dances, there can be a crude joke there, dancing with girls and looking at boys, realizing that both had potential, that both could be the subject of erotic inquiry; but also, everything in a moment could collapse into one moment of pleasure, pulled like toffee for two hours, especially in the middle of winter, but also in the summer. I wanted my body to feel other bodies next to me. I wanted loud music on shitty speakers bouncing off carpeted floors and walls. They had a diverse playlist and a DJ who worked a talk-radio gig on conservative radio. He played Stealers Wheel not knowing about *Reservoir Dogs* the same way he played 'Time Warp' without knowing about *Rocky Horror*. Boney M, without knowing how queer they were, plus Led Zeppelin without believing they were satanic. Once, the DJ pulled me aside, with a printed Excel spreadsheet and a pen. He asked me which songs didn't please the Lord. I was flattered that he trusted my taste as a critic and embarrassed that it was universally known that I had fallen short of the glory of God. Read as queer even then.

Part of the problem of hunger, or unsatiated curiosity, was thinking that I could have everything that I wanted without consequences. As I grew older, the control of adults in my life abated, and I didn't know which way I wanted to go. The missionaries could clear out my archive of decadence, and then the next week I could go to the used bookstore and buy more porn, or I could sneak off to a bar and listen to Johnny Cash in the middle of the day. I could go to gay youth groups on Friday night throughout Grades 10 and 11; then I could go to church dances on Saturday. I could attend lessons on converting to Catholicism during the week, and on the weekend book a trip to the temple. I could lie to the bishop and still think of myself as pious. Maybe that's what it means to be a teenager.

I was encouraged to leave the Mormons after Far West confessed to his boss about how I seduced him, and I left, sliding further into a kind of dissatisfied desire, the liquidity of my being fitting whatever container it could.

The dancing I did before I was eighteen was social dancing intended to contain wild adolescents, to provide them a good moral example, to keep them off the streets. Cock straining against my boxers, with no relief. There must have been queer kids in that room, must have been kids who discovered facts when they went on missions, or who married and then found out. I found out early – and I sometimes wished I could switch places. Before being sent away, I didn't know how to masturbate, how to fuck, how to suck or be sucked. At seventeen, in the middle of a church cultural hall, part of me wanted one of those boys who was about to go on his mission or had just come back. I wanted him to bring me to a dark room and pray for me, or I wanted him to bring me to the parking lot and fumble in the back seat of a too-small Camry. I wanted to see him on Sunday loudly singing the bass parts of the hymns, and I wanted him on the back forty bent over with his plaid shirt pulled up and his choring pants pulled down. Driving around on a Satur- day night, in a friend's parents' car (I never learned to drive), listening to the radio, talking and trying to retain purity, from small town to big city, that was its own escape I was absent from. The return to the farm as a sort of homecoming, also not possible for me.

I wanted other, more complicated, things. I knew that I was never going on a mission, so I would never be sealed in the temple. I would never marry at all. The church was to train for the domestic and had no idea how to handle those who would fail those tasks. If there was a desire to teach, and a desire to learn, that learning could be understood. If there was a desire to teach, and no desire to learn, then the kid who was being taught was just lazy. They could tell from the earliest age how much I tried to learn, but they did not know how to teach me – it wasn't the good boy gone bad, it wasn't even the moral distinction between being a good or bad kid, it was the inscrutable collection of adult hungers and adult desires gathering, rotting someone from the inside.

Dancing at these places: the seven minutes of 'Stairway to Heaven,' a frustrated broken rhythm that put the *dry* in dry humping; the four minutes of Savage Garden's 'Truly Madly Deeply,' with its odes to fidelity in a room where fidelity is so normative; or the three minutes of chaste modesty in Sixpence None the Richer's 'Kiss Me.' I aged out of virtue. However, nothing was more erotic to me than the wanting and not getting – another kind of violence perhaps, more internal, and less physical.

The missionary must have known that I was the kind of person who would have sucked him off without really asking. The elderly church DJ must have known that I was the kind of person to know all the dirty bits in all of the dirty songs. The only kid who was willing to suck someone off, the only kid who knew the filthy subtext, was in the room for all this purity.

As I grew older, as my world grew larger, I found other places to dance, and other places to find meaning, that lacked the ambivalence of the church. I spent my twenties going to these places – in Edmonton and Vancouver, at conferences in San Francisco and New Orleans, once in London. Places where I got tossed off in the bathroom and went back to the dance floor, places where I grinded against people, shirtless and slick with fluids, places where I followed people home, places where the ecstasy of dancing was placed in the context of the back-alley blow job or the hand job at the edge of an abandoned train station or in the taxi home.

When I was in my mid-twenties, I was at an academic conference in New Orleans. I spent Easter Sunday at a notorious leather bar, getting increasingly drunk. I was dancing to this angular abstract, minimal noise – just the bounce of the rhythm track. Someone dressed as the Easter Bunny came in and followed me to the washroom. He took off his gloves and he gave me a hand job. Another time, I went to the Eagle in the Castro and accidentally drank from a bottle on top of the urinal – not my long-neck Bud but a bottle of piss that someone had graciously left as a gift. None of these experiences would have happened without the church dances, or the hospital, or the boarding school, the restrictions of bodies and the loosening of bodies working in a concordance of permission seeking and rules keeping.

I think that in those spaces of my youth, plausible deniability had a certain power. I couldn't dance with the boys, but I could dance with the girls and look at the boys – the imagination liberated in ways that actual possibilities elsewhere didn't allow. The church dances were the place where both/and seemed both the most real and the most impossible.

The first time I came out, at fourteen, I used the word *gay* – denying all of the landscape that exists between both/and. I was going to tell a nurse I thought I could trust. So I sat down and thought a long while – and I considered in my heart the dancing with the girls from church, falling in love with the girls from church (wouldn't that have been easier?), then the slash widened and split me open. I thought about the punk gamine at the end of the hallway, of the gutter Marilyn on Seroquel in the room two doors down from me, the kid who tried to look like Angelina Jolie circa *Girl, Interrupted* and sort of succeeded – the locked ward of a psych facility had a range of types and all of them struck me as distinct possibilities. Different possibilities than the church girls, who took care of me; different possibilities than even the teachers and wives at boarding school. I was starting to fracture from my childhood. I was starting to recognize that I wouldn't be married, and I wouldn't have babies, and I wasn't sure what I wanted or what was next.

The little epicurean eventually won, but it took a long while. It took me a long while to realize how important my body was – that my body didn't want to be contained by gender or sex. My body wanted to be pogoing chaotically to mid-nineties safe punk, or falling to the ground with everyone at the end of 'Rasputin,' or moving to the rasp of the first scandalous lines of Nine Inch Nails' 'Closer,' or to Alanis Morrissette singing about what she would do in theatres, and leaning in to the handsome young missionary, whose diaphragm would retract and expand as he reached the baritone notes of 'Ye Elders of Israel.' A song sung louder and sloppier, more like a shanty than a hymn – it would be a bonding moment when I met a close friend in my first year of undergrad.

This was the highlight, the mid-nineties highlight, of sexual possibilities. I was angry but not angry in the way that Fred Durst was angry – I didn't want to break shit, as much as I wanted to break myself or be broken. I must have played Alanis a thousand times, imagining that I could be the person who went down on a man in a movie theatre. Years later, at the old Fox Cinema in Vancouver, I sat in the front row of that crumbling metroplex watching a vintage seventies 35 mm print, having a guy suck me off; and then years after that, a boyfriend trying to distract me with his mouth while I was trying to understand the intricate plot of Duncan Jones's *Moon*.

There were other aspirations: I didn't like my body, I didn't like having a body, this new body, this body that was growing hips and ass despite my desires, this body with its stomach that doubled over, this pigeon-toed body with arched back and clumsy affect. This masculine, bearded, full-bush body. The gender dysphoria, which began for me at eighteen, was not that I was read as a boy but was really a girl, or as a boy who was failing at being a boy, but that I had a body that I didn't want. There were contexts for the crossing and erasing of gender barriers but not precedent for a body that seemed to come alive only in the seeking of pleasure – the body that existed only as I came, or when the meal was done, or at the movies, or in a gallery, the body that retreated to a non-self-loathing place when it just had to exist. It helped to have a cadre of women musicians like Björk or PJ Harvey or Tori Amos who told me to have a body, that my unruly body should be kept unruled.

The church dances were intended to rule. When the boys would come back from missions, the girls would join them in the young single adult wards. A ritual, to separate them from their family and to find a worthy mate. Mormonism was about finding the potential for decadence in the midst of control. But we were not supposed to listen to the songs that would encourage or give succour to those desires; my collection of these cassettes had just been thrown out by the missionaries in an attempt at piety that eventually failed.

The control of the body, the body not feeling real, were universal themes. When Courtney Love sang that she was 'Doll Parts,' that distance from the body and how it was represented – the abstraction of my flesh into the incorporeal – well, that was part of it … But also, when I was told that my body was being punished again and again for being unruled, that I also had flesh, I also had a part of it. I was being told that I stood in ways that took up too much space, that I ate too much, that I read too much or spent too much money, or that my body was chaotic and proliferate, the church and the clinic working as twin agents to make me compliant – but then I had Courtney Love telling me about the legitimacy of pain, and that I could be the girl with the most cake, could be a girl, and more importantly could be a girl whose appetite could not be contained.

There were others: there was Bikini Kill, whose rebel girl suggested that the hips that I hated could be a source of rebellion, and when someone put his cock in my ass it wasn't shameful but sweet, that wanting my roommate to kiss me had distinct potential. There was that cover of *Rolling Stone* with Liz Phair, and the confusion about whether I wanted to fuck her or be her, and how that had its own distinct possibility – the sweet narcissism of wanting to fuck yourself, the radical potential of being a girl and being a boy and wanting to have the boys and wanting to have the girls and knowing without articulating that the landscape between boy and girl, between subject and object, was as dangerous, as all-consuming, as hot as the prairie on fire. Then there was Tori Amos, whose *Boys for Pele* was a little later but who suggested that the fear of divine condemnation was unjust. Then there was PJ Harvey.

All the things that I wanted to be, that I would never get to be, PJ Harvey was. PJ Harvey was Mick Jagger singing 'Sympathy for the Devil' in Hyde Park in 1969; she was James Brown singing 'Sex Machine' in Paris in 1971; she was the Elvis comeback special without ever having gone anywhere; she was Leonard Cohen on the Isle of Wight in 1970. I understood and was beguiled by her in ways that I was never beguiled by any boy, by any rock star. Listening to 'Sheela-Na-Gig' – the anthem of being told that you were much too much, and literally saying fuck it; having a man tell you that you have shown too much, and you respond, Look at my hips, look at my lips, look at my idle hole – pay me for my body, pay me for all of the absences that you have made present, make present that which is claimed by men to be absent. Not sex, not pussy or ass, she sings, but hips, a body part that I never liked, a body part that I have too much of (what does it mean to have child-bearing hips when you will never bear children – is this another split from the biological?) – the man afraid of the grime of his desiring, the body as a rejoinder to those who seek purity.

Then, at Glastonbury in 1995 (a performance I read about in *Spin*, or maybe saw on MuchMusic), she sings '50ft Queenie.' There is nothing more powerful to me than '50ft Queenie.' I hate my body. I hate the size and shape of my body, I hate how tall I am, how fat I am, how dumb my body is, how awkward and incapable of grace.

I hated my body in the ways that the church told me to hate my body, and the pagan heat of PJ Harvey at her most feral returned me to Babylon.

PJ Harvey talking about how her largeness is an overwhelming amount of sexual power, that her body controls itself through mass, how she says it by gliding over that stage, in front of ten thousand people, in a hot pink catsuit unzipped to her navel, revealing a black lace bra – that is the kind of swagger I want, the kind of exhibitionism I want.

A year before that performance, there was an issue of *Spin* with her on the cover. She is spectrally white, with hair black as the night, her breasts covered by a bra the same colour as her skin. The image has a haunting eroticism; she is staring straight at us, daring us to want, daring us to admit our appetite. It feels like an invitation to our own destruction. I had seen pornography at this point, in all varieties, with audiences and without, but this is the first time that I feel punctured, this is the first time that I feel the punctum of the erotic, the first time that something is so powerful that I am not sure of its utility.

Cracking me open, not yet to talk of the desire of gender transgression but thinking about the transgression of sex – even at fourteen, a lifetime of negotiation, of neglect and refusal, another twenty years of saying not yet, but at that moment, I say, Okay, this is me, this is who I want to be. I want to be Harvey's Queen.

So I tell this nurse, I say to that nurse, a mumbled and barely articulated version of this. She was kind when I told her I was maybe gay, but she turned a little cold when I told her I was more than that. I didn't use the word *bisexual*, or *pansexual*, or anything but that I wanted boys, and sometimes I wanted girls, and I am not even sure that I knew that there were worlds between boys and girls. What I wanted to say to her, I think, was that I wanted all the cake, and to never say no to cake ever again.

She told me I was confused. That I didn't know. That I should keep quiet, and severely, that it was a symptom or a set of symptoms, this confusion, that I needed to pay attention to who I was and what I wanted.

I wanted to be the girl with the most cake.

# Lesson Ten:
# Looking for a Daddy in All
# the Right Places

The Continental Baths in Edmonton were a place where men have congregated since the nineteenth century. They were close to the dive bars where country music played, and the adult theatres. I found them in the two years I was back home, back living with my mom and going to high school, after the ward, and though they weren't the nicest, they were cheaper and more convenient than the baths, closer to the subway. I must have known them from the closeness to the theatres – the theatres never sponsored the pride parade, they didn't put ads in the print publications, they didn't stock the weeklies either (there were six of them in Edmonton at one time). The theatres and the Continental were intended for men who had sex with men but who were not queer – the distinct taxonomy. Some sex places were for men who were queer, some sex places for men who enjoyed the convenience, some sex places for men alone; the list in your head, a Rolodex of very specific vices, was its own introduction into the social niceties of adult life.

The Times Square was in a square, brick building. One floor. The front had sex toys and videos; the back had video booths. Here's how it would work: you would give the front desk clerk five or ten bucks, and they would give you a handful of brass tokens lighter than but the same diameter as a loonie. You would find an empty booth, insert coins, and flip channels. The whole thing was a single integrated unit resembling the coin-operated TVs in the downtown bus station. If you left the door open a little bit, people would emerge from the fluorescent darkness and watch you. They would never talk. There would be pantomime, for you to touch, for them to touch. In the video booths, at the back, I learned more about consent and non-verbal communication than in any social skills class or occupational therapist's intervention. Edmonton is a town that is split by class, but during lunch hour, I'd have all kinds of men: mechanics from the garages still in coveralls, smelling like oil and cleaning fluid; minor bureaucrats in khaki trousers working carefully to preserve their tie from spunk; students playing hooky. I would go four or five times a year, taking inventory every time.

In the dirt-and-concrete-floored basement of one of those nineteenth-century buildings was the Centrefold. At the Centrefold, you would enter through the store and pass through a blackout curtain. At the Centrefold, you would either walk down a set of slat stairs or sneak through the back door. At the Centrefold, there would be a bank of four videos shown in a grid on your right. Beyond those four walls were stone walls and a painted concrete floor. Lit like a catacomb, smelling like bleach, the booths themselves were cobbled together; one might not even have had chairs. Most of the screens showed eighties porn, the grain preserved on digital transfer, but the digital transfer itself was kind of terrible – analog decay atop digital decay. One day, there were three videos like that, along with Neil Jordan's *The End of the Affair* in a crisp new print, its erotic melancholy offset with chic grey purples. Nothing sadder, nothing sexier in that moment than a fully clothed Julianne Moore.

I don't remember ever being greedy enough to have sex in more than one place in the same day. Cruising is a continued case of failing again better – if there was no one at the baths, or no one interested enough in me, I would go to the Centrefold. Sometimes at the Centrefold, jerking off in public was enough – but maybe the porn wasn't working for me, or the machines weren't working, or I wanted to jerk off in front of someone, or see someone else's cock, and so I would move on to the next place. Sometimes I struck out. Sometimes I just got bored.

Taking the bus down Jasper Avenue, past the bookstores, newsstands, far from the river – on the edge of a tiny neighbourhood called Oliver, in a strip mall, next to the first Earl's, there was a more modern bathhouse. That was the one I went to with money borrowed or taken from my mother. I developed a routine: newsstand, bookstore, cheap Chinese for lunch, a rye and ginger at one of the dives, and this bathhouse. It had thick vinyl runners, a properly contained entry counter, a mural of men together in a pool. The lighting was all on a dimmer, the viewing rooms had leather couches. Even the hot tub and sauna were not stand-alone units but built-in. There was no sign, no indication, of what happened in the basement. I don't remember the sex there very much. The sex I didn't have, or the sex I had quietly, is what returns to my memory. But there was a bus driver or two; at least one rig worker coming in from a week north of Fort McMurray, still smelling faintly of unrefined crude and the orange soap used to scrub it off; a local community leader; and sometimes, when I was really lucky, rednecks with thick northern accents – uncut, because they were born at home, or because to snip was more expensive.

Past Jasper Avenue and toward Stony Plain Road, there was a porn theatre, built later, and cleaner – the chairs bolted on, fibreglass injection moulded. It was two blocks from a Goodwill, across from a used bookstore with a rack of vintage gay porn mixed in with old *Playboys* and *Penthouses*. The little digest ones were my favourites: first-person stories, published by First Hand Tales of Teaneck, New Jersey. It was safer and cleaner than the other places, lower key. The glory holes had pieces of PVC pipe placed tightly in the walls, a smooth place to rest fingers or cocks. I still needed to see a face, touch the top of a head as someone was going down on me, or needed to look up with thankful eyes and be patted on my head like I was a hungry lab doing a rare trick (pun not intended). Even at its most anonymous – in bathhouses, in the backrooms of porn theatres, in public washrooms – the etiquette of the glory hole escaped me. But they had their own grammar, their own rhetoric, even their own collapsing of sign and signifier. A finger would emerge, trace the circle around the hole, a finger would reciprocate, and then a cock would emerge. When the straight pornographer Nicholson Baker wrote a book about transtemporal phase shifting and science-fiction orgasms and called it *House of Holes*, it felt like he was adding all of that literary signification to those brief encounters.

The second Times Square location was four or five blocks from the Centrefold. Two blocks from the art school with the good library, a block from the Burger Baron (a trash fast-food chain that had milkshakes, corn fritters, and Hawaiian burgers) and a block from another strip mall, but more modern, most likely from the late 1960s or 1970s. Less of a mix of white- and blue-collar, almost exclusively blue. The whole place was huge and blank – Formica counters and linoleum floors. Spunk smells like bleach, and they would clean spunk with bleach; linoleum holds a smell well. The booths were in the back, blond plywood, hastily constructed, no care and no paint. The people who went there were more aggressive, had less of the do-si-do of other sex, more willing to invade spaces, less willing to take no for an answer. It was the only place where you could rent a video to preview in the booths. But I had the internet, and I didn't need help.

Just after I finished high school, I went to a job-search organization – one of those make-work projects where they got government funding based on how many certificates you got and how many jobs you applied for. One of the porn shops I had visited was advertising for a front desk clerk. I was going to apply, but the organization didn't want to acknowledge it. They wouldn't drop me off, they wouldn't help me prep a resumé or an interview for the place. I needed to apply to a certain number of jobs to keep in the program, and keeping in the program would help me get some money from the government, but applying to porn shops would not aid in these quests. I put in an application anyway – partly because I didn't see the difference between renting videos at a Blockbuster and at a Centrefold, partly because I didn't want to be a hypocrite, and partly because I got off on the idea of the Chris Isaak–looking section leader imagining me working at a porn shop.

While I was dropping off my application, a man walked into the backroom. He was one of the most handsome people I had ever seen (he is still one of the most memorable). I didn't follow him back, I remained professional, in my thrift-store button-up and my Army and Navy dress pants. If I had gone back, maybe the sex would have been good enough to remember; or it would have been terrible; or it might not have happened at all. The spirit of Walt Whitman is best shown in spaces where nothing happens, or where something happens that might not be what you want, or in the temporary butterfly joy of it happening just once. I still think of that man, the half-a-second glimpse I had of him, walking past the powder-coated steel into the backroom. My desire for him has lasted longer than most other memories and has returned to me once a week.

# Lesson Eleven:
# Cowboy Takes Me Away

Lorelei James writes cowboy smut, branded as romance, with headless torsos clad in plaid emblazoned on her covers. It's smut, and unapologetic smut. Her books have titles like *One Night Rodeo, Wrangled and Tangled, Saddled and Spurred*, and *Corralled*. The last is my favourite – it features Hank and Kyle agreeing with Lainie to share each other's lives for a season. Kyle and Hank are best friends, and Lainie is a sports therapist. The cowboys are rough men who do rough things to Lainie; they have an edge of patriarchal violence, but in their agreement there is some conversation, and consent, most of it implied. Cowboy novels often have the cowboys die violent deaths or never fuck each other or run off into the sunset or fail to be good people – it's unfortunate that James's cowboys never fuck each other. Romance novels are sort of like comedy in that they usually end with a wedding, and they don't veer too far from expected sexual patterns, though there may be some riffs before the end of the book. James is brilliant because she keeps the tease going for so long. Reading the work, and shuffling through the characters as they fuck together, then apart, and waiting for Kyle and Henry to fuck, returns you to the nostalgic haze where you think that the boys will finally get together – and so the disappointment is even harsher when they don't.

The fantasies in James's novels are about the middle ground between being taken care of and being taken advantage of. The sex is carefully described – somewhere between the 'mean masculine chuckles' and making sure that the clit is being paid attention to, somewhere between the switching sides and the careful noticing of how much pleasure Lainie is getting, the cruelty is enfolded with a softer desire, or the softer desire is made spikier by excerpts that include rope play or horse play or other accessories, reminding me of the kink adage that it's cheaper to find gear in a tack shop than in a sex shop.

Reading contemporary erotic literature – I'm thinking especially of the sex tourism of Garth Greenwell's *Cleanness* – where what we have is a pure cruelty, where accuracy is mirrored in cruelty: to be real is to be mean. *Cleanness* is about having amoral sex in post-Soviet tower blocks. The sex is degrading, the buildings are degrading, the desire is degrading, and because it can be hidden as some kind of metaphor for class tourism or economic collapse or economic exploitation, it can be taken seriously. Reading Greenwell is to be taught; reading James is playing hooky from being taught. Of course, all sex is trans-actional, but that doesn't mean it can't be fun.

I read James because I want two cowboys to fuck me; I read James because I want to read about women being fucked well and often by men, and that's weirdly hard to come by; I read James because I can fit myself into the narrative, imagine myself as Lainie. I also read James because she reminds me of places that no other writer has ever really placed into context. James writes about motels really well. The American novelist James Salter wrote the one fuck book that mainstream critics have decided is good enough to be in the literary canon, and it takes place in a hotel. Salter describes furniture really well, but the hotel is in France and the furniture is expensive *objets*. James writes about the cheap motels on the sides of highways – she describes the kind of working-class sex, of staying up nights in those motels and watching porn and talking, that feels current and present.

When Kyle and Hank are talking about how to share Lainie (I know that phrase is problematic), they talk about how the motels work, how rodeo cowboys live in those motels, next door to one another. Then they talk about not sucking each other's cocks, talk about the intricacies of sharing, talk about what they want, and they talk about Lainie. They talk while drinking in the parking lot of these motels, and even how the parking lot is discussed is central – how horse trailers park at the edges of dark lots, the sound of beer bottles hitting the truck bed or the pavement, sleeping in parking lots because one is too tired to be in a motel. They share this whole ecosystem of parking lots, parade grounds, highways, and cheap motels – an ecosystem that grows sexual potential in very distinct patterns.

James knows how long it takes to get to Cheyenne from any number of Great Plains sites; she knows that Cheyenne is the centre of cowboy culture. For James, it is both the idea of the place and the place itself – Cheyenne holds the largest and most historically significant rodeo in the West, centres erotic and social energy in one town for one week once a year. James is writing, perhaps accidentally, the great novel of Cheyenne. (It's useful to compare the hardness of her writing about sex with the soft, courtly waltz of George Strait's *I Can Still Make Cheyenne*, about a rodeo star who just made the big show, or

Pistol Annies' slower and less courtly ballad 'Cheyenne,' where a woman named after the city sleeps through 'pool table cowboys.') James writes about Cheyenne with a tenderness usually reserved for sex – just as she writes about the parking lots of motels, she writes about the give and take of the back lots of rodeo sites, the backstage mechanics that are absent from so much writing about the West. She writes about landscape.

James's book works because the motel is part of the work, because she knows how to slide between real estate – between the ranch, the barn, the home, the hotel, the motel, between all kinds of labour, all kinds of pleasure, all kinds of ways of being in the world.

———

Just after high school, I spent six months screwing a rodeo cowboy through Central Alberta. The rodeo cowboy in question was short but broad-shouldered and broad-chested. His hair was thick and tousled; between the ball caps and the Stetsons, the hair was mostly errant cowlicks. He had no acne, no scars or pits in his face. His ears stuck out. He shaved his face once a week on Sunday mornings, before church. Once or twice, he had a moustache, but for no longer than a week or two – once to play a cop on Halloween, once as a joke before a buddy's wedding. My favourite time to kiss him was Friday because I love beard against stubble, friction like kindling. He wore tight white T-shirts and Western-cut overshirts when he was feeling formal, work shirts when he wasn't. He wore T-shirts from his 4H days, or from John Deere giveaways, or from small-town hockey tournaments, to go to bed. He didn't trim his chest hair or under his arms and he had a thick enough pelt to grab on to when he was fucking you. His hands could cover your whole ass and twist your tits – so little finesse, so much necessary roughness. He wore tight Wranglers or thick Carhartts. A brown leather belt three fingers thick. Once or twice, he hit you with the belt; once or twice, he hit you with his hand. The belt had a buckle he'd won– he was never a good bull rider, but he was stubborn enough to last eight seconds or so every so often. He had a little hairless gully, cum-gutters slashing down to a perfect cock. Parents too poor to circumcise, thick as my thumb, wide enough for my thumb and forefinger to stretch. Between those Wranglers and that cock, tight Fruit of the Looms, loose boxers, depending on whether it was a laundry day. The boxers were a plaid flannel, one pair red, one pair blue. The crotch stretched out, the elastic saggy, a hole near the lower thigh. His ass was as high and tight and wide as two hills on the prairie, whiter than bleached Sunday shirts. The colour and the dimples, and the downy hairs, almost a gosling. He wore workboots, steel-toed, and didn't have a pair of the needle-toed cowboys. Tiny feet, though – dancers' feet. He smelled like English Leather cologne, sweat, cheap toothpaste, horseshit, leather, and mentholated salve.

The smell is the longest memory, and one that hits the hardest. There is much less detail in James's novels about how smell stops, how it descends into class, how it is about work. Reading James write about Hank: 'Just once he would like him to smell natural, no sweet-smelling soap, just the raw, salty, dark taste of Hank.'

I liked the smell of my cowboy because it was in competition. The rodeo was a burlesque of actual farm labour, but being with him was something more real: thinking about my nose in his armpit, in his full bush, in his ass – there was always the salt and the dark, umami smell of flesh. Humans civilize ourselves, we hide the sweat, but the sweat always wins – the body reasserts itself, there is nothing entirely natural and nothing feral, but the feral and the natural competing – so the soap doesn't work to hide the sweat, and the salve doesn't work to hide the piss, and the toothpaste doesn't hide the cigarettes from the night before or the chaw in the morning; nothing covers up the leather or the horseshit. The man rides the bull, the man rides me, the soap rides the man, the bull and the horse and the soap and eventually maybe me become a little bit raw – but like oysters are raw but also cooked, so sophisticated in their rawness, so is my cowboy. When I suck him off well enough, when he cums, it doesn't seem an accident that his cum tastes like an oyster, this man so far from the sea, and the raw/cooked/feral/civilized food deep within him. The sweetness of the soap only deepens the sourness of the rest.

We met at a barn dance. I was a year out of school, on a security gig for the dance after the farm fair, and he was placed at the edge of the money, and for the next two months or so, we slept together often and not well.

We didn't sleep together when I was on the job, but I went back to the fair during my time off – not to see him as much as to spend time watching the rodeo. I didn't approach the boys who clustered around the chute, and I didn't stay later than the Greyhound ran. Once, I risked it and went to the dance after the rodeo. There were boys clustered on the edges of the room, and another set by the bar – more men than women. I sat on the edge of the floor and watched. I tried to remember the steps to 'Cadillac Ranch' when the line dancing started, but that didn't go very well. It got later and later, the boys went home with their wives, or sometimes with a girl, and toward the end, there were half a dozen of us. I hadn't talked to anyone all night, and I didn't know how I was going to get home. It was long past midnight, almost last call. I stretched my legs, went for a piss, and looked for the pay phone. No one was around, and there he was. He hadn't left with any of the girls, though he was handsome enough, and he didn't pack with the boys, just looked me over with a side eye – sort of cruising, sort of negotiating the differences between danger and safety.

I don't remember how the Cowboy brought up that he wanted to sleep with me. I think maybe he saw me in the uniform and knew that I would have gotten fired if I had told – but it was a shit job, and if I lost it, I would have landed on family money of some form or another, so I didn't need it. I wonder, if I had told anyone, if he would have stopped sleeping with me, which would have been bad, or if he would have hit me or kicked me with a certain vigour, which would have been a bonus. None of this was well thought out, or considered, before our first encounter.

He was a few rye and gingers in, and led me from the rodeo dance to the cluster of ad hoc chutes and stalls behind the arena. The boys who set up for the rodeo were home for the night and we were alone. He turned left and right. Past the animals bedded for the night, past the trailers and camps where the support staff were hanging out, snaking further and further into the dark. He found a stall that had been there for a while – made of creosoted wood, a permanent fixture. Alan Jackson was playing in the distance. I was taller than him, but he commanded that space. Wanting a quiet place to talk, I wasn't sure what was going to happen next. He didn't talk much. He was dressed for the dance after the rodeo (work wear, rodeo wear, dance wear, another thing I would learn with him, another kind of etiquette) – wearing a new Stetson, and he didn't want to get it messed with horseshit, muck, and dust. He pulled me into the corner of that pen, further and further from the sound of the crowds. He took my hand in the near dark, splayed my fingers out with his hands, one by one, like loosening a fist; he grabbed my fist and led that loose fist over his crotch. Tight grip on my wrist, grinding my hand into the denim.

The hat brim prevented my moving closer, the hand against my wrist prevented me from leaning in. He shoved me against the paddock, he bucked his hips toward my hips, he leaned back, and for a hot minute it was just denim against denim. Riding me like he rode other animals – not very good, but eager and fast. He reached up to grab my hair. He pulled my hair toward him, a whole hunk of it almost pulling out. I leaned forward into his pulling. He growled into my ear. *Down, now.* My knees sunk into the mud, he climbed to the second rail of the paddock fence.

We were celebrating the new buckle, the clang of it against the buttons of his fly. He shoved his cock out of his pants and pushed my head onto it. I engulfed the whole thing. He stunk, no time to clean. Too eager. My cock straining and my back straining, and my hands trying to get balance, and my neck and throat against him. Neither letting go. A rider learns to work with a bull but I'm not a bull here. He shoves further and faster until he spurts into my mouth.

He pulled his cock back out from between my teeth. Cleaning his hands with a fresh blue bandana, he tells me to get up, we walk silently back to the party. After a few more songs he drives me to where I am staying – a room with no kitchen and no bathroom, in the basement of a house in the postwar suburbs.

A few weeks later he invited me to the strip club in the basement of the Coliseum Inn on a Saturday night. Not the classy one on the south side, the one across Northlands, where the Oilers used to play and where the rodeo was. He was having a really good night. He had placed in the money; no one let him pay for beers all night; his favourite girls were on the main stage shaking tits to Bocephus and Garth ('Friends in Low Places,' an oddly popular song in the clubs in those years). He won a little dosh at the slots. He was feeling magnanimous and wanted to show off his good fortune to me, not for me. He was too sloppy to get home, almost too sloppy to get upstairs.

For me, the reverie is the reverie of prairie hotels, which exist in my history but do not exist in places that I have written or read about. Fucking the Cowboy in an Edmonton or Ponoka hotel was the introduction to more disappointing or less considered sex. A boy can suck your cock, and any hole is the goal, but a boy sucking your cock in a hotel room, well then, he's committed.

He slid me enough money for a room, the one left on the top floor, and told me to meet him up there. My credit card didn't have enough (any) money on it, but the fistful of cash made up enough for the extra deposit. It might have been twenty minutes, might have been an hour, before I heard the rustle of the key in the lock. He stumbled into the room with a woman behind him, a six-pack in one hand, his other wrapped around her waist. He had stuffed a mickey of Alberta Premium Rye in his waistband. Introductions were made, the cowboy slurring, asking if we were ready for a good time. I left the room to get ice, and by the time I was back, his shirt was half off, his undershirt exposed, his boots half off, his belt unlaced from a few loops. The woman he was with had her T-shirt in the corner, red bra exposed.

He told me to kneel at the head of the bed. She settled into the middle, and he stood firm at the edge. Off the bed. The three of us had the full range of clothing options, none of us fully naked, none of us with very good coordination. She undid my zipper, dragging out my cock with her bright red nails, plopping its still soft form into her mouth.

He dropped his boxers, slid her panties to the side. There was not a lot of conversation. He pumped with the efficiency of a car needing a tire change. I kept sipping my drink until I was close, and then put it down. I extended my arms against the full length of the plastic wood headboard, pushed down with my full palms. I looked at her back, looked at him, looked down at her face, and bucked a little, looking back at him. He exited just before he came and finished on the polyester bedspread.

I came a minute later, tapping her on her shoulder, saying I was ready. She rolled over, looking at the cowboy, then looking at me, three knuckles deep, finishing herself with the same efficiency.

I took a shower, and then they took a shower. Not doing much good, as we were wearing the clothes from the night before. They both had a beer and I finished up my paper cup of rye. The sun was rising against the plastic yellow of the sign. He gave me another fifty and told me it was cab fare.

I was the most sober one in that room. I was the one with the least money. I don't know if the fifty was cab fare, and he didn't know how much a cab was. I didn't know her name. I never saw her again. I could only articulate my own desire in the shape of his. This was the first woman I ever fucked, the first pussy I ever saw up close, and I saw it as a kind of conquest for a dumb cowboy who wanted to impress me and who I wanted to impress. There is a line between sleazy and a good time – this was sleazy. I knew I wanted more of it, I wanted more hotel rooms, more sweat, more unseamed beds, and more women. I wanted to taste pussy, and I wanted to taste cock, and I wanted that cowboy to grind and buck against me like I had a pussy, like he grinded against that horse.

He took care of me, but the magnanimity was about his own ego – the paying for the booze or the room or the cab home. The slots were loose, the horse rode well, he had cash in his pocket, the cash flowed in, and the cash flowed out. Flow was it: ride your boy with the flow of the horse, ride your body with the flow of the other body in your bed that night, and your flow and the body's flow would result in reward. He shared money like he shared his cock – because he wanted people to be surprised at its size.

I didn't know who I was, and I wasn't convinced that I was what the cowboy wanted – I wasn't a boy, I wasn't a girl, I wasn't a top, I wasn't a bottom, all I wanted was mouths all over me, and my mouth all over them. I was clumsy and ambivalent about my body, and this strutting creature had all the confidence I wanted.

He called me again, a few months later (he called, and I never called), and told me that he was riding in Ponoka, a big rodeo as far as the ones in Central Alberta went. He wanted me to come down, to see him ride. I thought this was the moment that I went from a hot call in the middle of the night to something resembling a boyfriend.

Like an idiot, I was on a Greyhound to Red Deer without a hotel or a way to get from there to Ponoka. The biggest event in a city of twelve thousand or so, the population would almost double that weekend, and rooms had been sold out for months. I thought he would take care of me, though there was no evidence of that before this moment.

I had no idea how to get hold of him. He moved often, some days living with his folks, though he only told me this in a less sober moment, explaining why he couldn't have me over. He stayed with friends every so often, but they couldn't know who I was, so I didn't know where he was. There were moments he would call me from the hotel, when he was on a construction job, or when he was riding somewhere. He talked about a girl he had just met when we went for dinner once, but never mentioned her again.

After the threesome he'd called a few more times. The Cowboy and I had fucked twice at this point, once in the middle of a field and once with someone else at a sleazy motel. I didn't drive. Even if I did drive, I didn't have a car. I didn't know how to hitchhike and didn't know if there was a bus from Red Deer to Ponoka. All I knew was that there was a grade-A fuck somewhere in Central Alberta and that I might be able to get some of it.

I had three hundred dollars in my account. A cab would have taken half of it. The pay phone in the bus station had a phone book, which included nearby towns. I was lucky: the phone book had all its pages. I called motels in Ponoka and asked if they had rooms. There was one for one night, at a place called Dino's, for about twice what it should have gone for. Someone had cancelled late Thursday. If I could be there in an hour, they'd hold the room.

There is this pulp novel called *Confessions of a Married Man*, published in 1969, that is a chronicle of every place this prep-school fellow has sex, from fourteen to forty, when he begins to discover his bisexuality. The book trades monologues from this person to interventions or questions from the psychiatrist. There is this moment where the prep tells a story about sliding down south, hitchhiking with a friend, from Virginia to New Orleans, where he moves from having sex with women to men and then back again. In one of those passages, a sailor picks him up in the French Quarter, they go to a hotel room, and there is another sailor there, the two sailors exchange bodies and affection with the prep, who is new to what he wants – being able to do this kind of work of the body, in a hotel room, is pleasure but is also identity.

At the hotel, I looked repeatedly through the rodeo program for the name he was born with and the name he rode with. I looked out the window, I watched more TV, and that afternoon, I went to the rodeo. I sat in the grandstands. I waited and waited – finally the riding events. He showed up as a late entry and drew a bad bull. He didn't make his eight seconds. It was a rough tumble. The medics came out and took him out of the arena.

The medic thought that I was family or a friend or someone close. I wonder if she thought we were together. He had his wallet and his keys in a plastic bag. On the ride back to the hotel, me in the front, him laid out in the back of a crew cab, sitting up so his head was nearest me and his feet were nearest the medic. His feet were in socks, his boots had to be removed to wrap an ankle. His shirt was half cut off to check on a rolled shoulder. He could have done a lot more damage. He was staying on the second floor while I was on the first. He was zonked on painkillers, but between the medic and I, we managed the wide steps to the second floor.

We went around the back, me taking his right side, the medic taking his left, and led him up surreptitiously. We got to the room; I laid him on his side on the bed farthest from the window. We were the farthest away from anyone else, my room was closest. We got him out of his clothes and helped him in the shower. He was smaller than me, but muscle is heavier than fat, and it took some effort to make sure that his abraded thighs and calves were carefully cleaned out.

After the medic left, I got him back into his bed, half-clothed, sort of objecting and sort of thankful, not knowing how I had gotten there or what I wanted. He told me to leave, that he would call me if he wanted anything. I slipped my hand between his thighs, four fingers resting on his fundament, and said that I wanted him to feel better. He swatted my hand away, told me to leave again. I spent a long night alone, back in my room, listening to the party outside, trying to read, trying to watch TV, wanting and not wanting to go back to his room.

As the party was dying down, I heard his voice outside my door. Telling the people left that he was doing okay, that the medic had brought him back because she was in love with him, that he didn't know who was in the front of the truck, that I must be a local working for extra money. He had one beer, then two, more Romeo talk, more talk about women, both in a code that I didn't really understand. I heard him describe the encounter at the Coliseum Inn, eliding my involvement entirely. The boys asked if he needed help getting back to his room, and as he said no, they wandered off – not believing him but not wanting to intercept his stoicism. I heard everyone leave one by one, pouring themselves into cabs, wandering back to their rooms.

I heard him struggle to get up, and so I opened the door to my room. I saw him half-leaning against a concrete retaining wall that marked the edge of the parking lot. I dragged him into my room, opiates and booze never a good match, and as with the rest of the day, I was in way over my head. I had to be out of the room by eight.

He passed out in the bed nearest the door, barefoot, pants dipping below his waist, shirt askew, crescent moon of hairy belly visible. I watched him sleep for a bit, memorized his body for future sessions, before going to bed myself. He was up by six. He had called the clerk and paid for my room for two more days. Told me he would find a way for me to be home by Sunday. His plan was for me to take his room at the top of the stairs, at the end of the quiet hallway – and he would stay in the room I had rented nearer the parking lot. He moved his duffle to my room. Told me to take a shower, to go to the local discount store and buy some clothes, to go to the co-op and get some basic groceries. Then stay in the room, killing time, waiting for him.

It's past nine when I can hear the party from the forecourt renew itself louder on Saturday than it was on Friday. I hear 'Boot Scootin' Bootie' and 'Watermelon Crawl,' I hear 'Are You Sure Hank Done It This Way' and 'A Country Boy Can Survive.' I finally realize that the Nitty Gritty Dirt Band's 'Fishin' in the Dark' is not about catching bass after midnight. The music comes from mix tapes and burned CDs on cheap stereo systems in expensive trucks. The bass is too heavy, and sometimes there is a boom box where there is no treble at all. I am sitting in the dark, watching shadows half dance, trying to get in the odd two-step.

It's long past midnight when the cowboy knocks on my door – three sharp knocks.

He's hanging on the lintel, half able to stand up, with a take-out cup of rye and ginger dangling from his left hand. His shirt is damp across his back, his fanciest shirt, the shirt he wore when we first met. We get undressed with a furious efficiency. I kneel on the floor and cradle his foot against my cock. The boot pushes down, crushing my hard-on into my belly, letting it rest there leaning into his foot so that my belly and my hips bracket the hardness of his boots. He leans over, whispers into my ear: *Does my little boy like when Daddy's rough?*

I stretch back, take his boot off, and repeat the gesture. I am aching, and dripping.

I'm wearing jeans and nothing else, the head of my cock painfully pushing against the Wrangler's brass zipper. I watch him piss, wash his hands, drag his own hands through hair and against the flesh. He looks at me looking and uses two fingers to beckon me over. I crawl on my hands and knees across cheap carpet to cool tile. He tells me to lean over the sink, drags down my pants.

I want that promise of his roughness, but he never delivers. He's not tender either. I go to work on his cock but he has a bad case of brewer's droop, and nothing I can do helps. He gets up. Cuffs my ears a bit and stumbles to the bathroom with the door open.

His body is against my body, his cock finally rising, he grabs my tits and is rough against them. He turns me around and grabs my cock and his cock in one hand, like two hands on the lead rein. Looking with a surprising directness, eye to eye, he roughly tosses me off, and when he's done, asks me to clean him up – with my mouth, a clean flannel, and not much else. He stumbles to the bed and passes out, as clumsy as he ever was.

The housekeeper's job is to be discreet – the rodeo weekend must be a tough gig, the rooms thick with sweat, with piss, with sweet sour empty beers and half cups of whisky, with horseshit – in a hundred rooms of spills and leaks, could one notice the differences between smells? If one does not need to pay attention, is it just endless riffs of the animalistic? The flannel was not clean, neither were the towels or the sheets, but were they any more or less unclean than those in the rest of the rooms? Different pleasures, same mess.

In the morning he wakes up and tells me to change and get dressed. He drives me in his pickup truck to Red Deer. About ten minutes into the ride, while still driving, he nods down to his crotch and tells me that his buddy needs attention; 120 km/h on the highway into town, I unzip him, try to make him proud. He's finished in a few minutes between Ponoka and Blackfalds, between the edge of one town and the next one, at risk of being caught. I am thinking of the Farmer all the way – of him in Blackfalds, him catching us, of the Cowboy being the Farmer. I clean him up again, this time with a travel package of Kleenex. I finish on his belly; the cum's lustre makes the perfect accessory to the pearlite buttons.

At Red Deer, the Cowboy gives me a little money for food and incidentals, a little more for the bus ticket, and sends me home.

I see him a few more times throughout Central Alberta, once in Calgary: the same ambivalent phone calls and hidden motel rooms, in places with names like the Sportsman, the Siesta, the Flamingo – they must all be gone now. Eventually, he invites me to the final dance of the Wetaskiwin rodeo. I don't have to invite myself. We don't dance, and I am stuck in a corner, just killing time again. Eventually, he leads me to the back stalls – close enough that we can hear the cattle lowing and the horses' muffled snorting. His sigh as he finishes has the same tone.

Dave Hickey, the Outlaw songwriter in seventies Austin, turned gallerist in the same town, turned art critic, turned Vegas academic, wrote an essay/moral fable about Hank Williams. There is a passage in that essay where Williams is driving somewhere between the northeast and southwest. He goes to a diner, and in the storeroom the waitress gives Hank a blow job. Hank finishes on his white flannel suit, and as he goes back to the car, he notes that the more money you have, the easier it is to clean up. He means this literally, taking out a little kit, which has the soap needed to clean semen out of a good Western suit, but also money gets awkward people and awkward situations out quicker too.

I thought the Cowboy loved me and was trying to protect me, but now past forty, I figure that he was trying to get me to leave. I don't know if I am the cum or the flannel or the little kit of soap in this metaphor, but I do know that he would pay for me to arrive, and he would pay for me to leave – and that old money reason for hiring sex workers (you don't pay for the sex, you pay for them to leave) comes into my head – naive little bugger, literally.

# Lesson Twelve:
# Text Becomes Flesh

You do a thing, or things, and you like a thing or things, but you live in a small town, and even if the librarian knows who you are, you can't say it out loud. You read compulsively, with hunger – reading as a distraction for the body, reading as a way of moving away, gulping information as fast as it comes, reading in order to formulate an escape plan. My favourite book as a child featured a family in East Germany clandestinely building a hot air balloon and floating to the other side of the wall. One of my favourite movies was *Return to Oz*, the nightmarish corrective of the 1930s original. I read books to narrativize a life that wasn't mine but I hoped would be. I finally found Ginsberg and carried his collected around like a totem, and then I found Frank O'Hara and carried his collected around like a totem. (I still have my high school edition of O'Hara, spine cracked, pages falling out, unreadable in its current state.) I bought those little Faber and Fabers, of *Ariel*, of *Boss Cupid*; I had Penguins of Muriel Spark.

I fucked and read about fucking. The avant-garde pornographer Dennis Cooper was hired by magazines like *Spin* or *Details*; the books were hard to get, but his profiles of soft boys who wanted to hurt me were fairly available. Samuel R. Delany's science-fiction was often out of print, but handsome editions of his memoirs about public sex were easier to find, and the very early Semiotext(e) books were small enough to put in a coat pocket.

When I first read Cooper or Ginsberg or Delany or Hervé Guibert or even Califia or Acker – sometimes autobiographical, sometimes not – they were stories about an adult who tries to or succeeds in having sex with someone younger, or an older person writing about how younger people have sex with each other; the view of it is always top down. Maybe that little bit of Delany's *Times Square Red, Times Square Blue* is more horizontal, the one where he is in a porno theatre in Times Square and he has someone blow him, and a few times, over a few years, as he goes back, they see each other, develop a relationship – and then they don't see each other for a few years, eventually running into each other in a bar when we discover (as Delany suspects) the assignations happened younger than someone admitted. But you don't often get a kid writing about the queer spaces that they shouldn't be in. I keep thinking about this when I read Guibert – I think about a lot of things when I read him. I think of his diaries, where everything seems made up and everything seems real; or when I read *To the Friend Who Did Not Save My Life* expecting all the gossip and, instead, getting a heartbreaking analysis of the aesthetics of mourning. I read his journals, and there is some conversation about pleasure, but nothing explicit; there is some conversation about sexuality, but nothing that would be outside of Gide or Cocteau, and more importantly, nothing that has not been found in his novels. This was Paris in the eighties, so the politics were left, but not that outré, and often the politics were subtle, interpersonal, more about the nuance of a heavily localized scene. In the 1970s there was an effort to liberate all kinds of sexuality, and an idea that anyone who impedes that liberation is reactionary. Those writers, including Foucault and Barthes and others, did not spend much time considering that liberation for one person could be oppression for another – that their appetites were caught in the power matrix that they were so concerned with.

We are not supposed to be sympathetic to the people who abuse us. We are supposed to treat them with horror and not tenderness. We are supposed to ritualistically speak against what is obvious. As an adult, I see my teenage years as this effort to eat everything that was set in front of me, to be wild, and to resent the adults who punished me for my ferality. I did dangerous things in those years – grasping, desperate, dangerous things.

Precocious children who are isolated or bored of childhood think that they are adults, and there are adults who want to treat them like it. There needs to be a moment when a child is in a room where they shouldn't be and the adults say, *You have been charming for this limited amount of time, but adults are doing adult things now, and those adult things are not for you.* The hunger that the child has for adult things beyond their understanding must be noted and must be put away.

When I consider the problems of my desire, or of desire in general, when I notice that I am drowning in these desires, I return back to French theory, which seems both blunter and more finessed than other sources. I think about Barthes, whose *A Lover's Discourse: Fragments* is about family, about reading, about eating, and about sex, about placing all those things within the cultural context where he was living, his daily life, but also about German novels from the nineteenth century and other critics from the twentieth century. Barthes would write small notes in the margins of a text that was already mostly fractured notes – there was something charming and calming and loving about a note in the margin of a margin. Guibert wrote, a decade after Barthes's sudden death, his theory matching Barthes's fracturing, his praxis not refracted but laser focused, not on endless subjects of desire across animal, mineral, or vegetable, but on only one or two or, at the most, six humans.

I return to Guibert, who glosses Barthes and befriends Foucault. I hope that Guibert will teach me a way through my desires, my all-consuming hunger, how theory slides into praxis, repeatedly.

Even at his most theoretical, Guibert supplies a way forward – his book of photography a tender gloss on Barthes – also hinting at sex, but never quite delivering. Then, I found a copy of his auto-theory *Crazy for Vincent*. Vincent was fifteen. Vincent might be real; Vincent might be invented. Guibert died before he was forty, of AIDS.

The critic, essayist, and curator Charlie Fox includes Guibert's *Vincent* in a canon of 'fucked-up boy art' – including on that list Caravaggio's painting 'Young Sick Bacchus,' Anne Carson's *Autobiography of Red*, and 'Larry Clark's entire career.' This is a very 1990s canon. These are the references that marked my ambition. The abject made a comeback and I wanted all that comeback – but I wasn't a fucked-up little boy. I wore emerald smoking jackets and pearls in high school, I painted my nails silver after I read Isherwood, I went to Europe for the first time and came back with volumes that were not published in America, but I was never a fucked-up boy. The educational assistants, the nurses, the doctors, the occupational therapists, the church elders – they had protocol for a fucked-up boy, but they didn't have protocol for the kind of fuck-up I was. (Guibert: 'I had wanted to slip so many skins on Vincent: that of a whore, that of a child, that of a thug, that of a sadist, that of just anyone.')

I wanted to be skinned and reskinned like Guibert wanted to do to Vincent, skinned and reskinned like avatars, like cybernetic selves, like post-flesh beings, like the cyberpunk new utopia that was fed to us as a kind of new flesh. I never got that.

Vincent had power in Guibert's imagination, and Vincent took all that power, consumed all of it as much as he could. Reading *Vincent* in my forties, I see the excuse-making and game-playing of me as a teenager, and I diagram who is confessing what to whom. When I was seventeen, I realized that sometimes saying faux naïf things out loud got me what I thought I wanted. In one example, on a Greyhound bus from Edmonton to Vancouver, I had a young Baptist pastor tell me how not to masturbate, and later I would masturbate to that negation – in the same spirit, my grasp for piety brought Far West into my mouth, and maybe convinced the Dorm Master I was a worthy target.

It is flattering when you are twelve or fifteen to be told that you have enough erotic power to make a man lose his will, his countenance, everything that makes him an adult – to spend too much money, to spill too much seed. And there is a kind of elegant agony when you, at fifteen, see the other kids – who are smaller, blonder, sleeker, more cynical or more jaded, or more able to pass – pretend not to be hungry. When I was fifteen, going into the city, going into places to fuck, I looked like I was twenty – I never looked fifteen. I remember telling a parent of a kid a couple summers ago about being neurodivergent and growing up weird, that I never wanted to be a kid, never thought of myself as a kid, just waited it out until I could pretend otherwise.

This is of course about the Dorm Master.

I know that the Dorm Master must have realized that I was a queer kid and that he exploited my queerness – that however uneven my memories of the events in the duty master room are, I had desire, and I thought about the Dorm Master in a sexual manner. That when a penis enters a mouth, a penis meets a hand, the practical emerges from the theoretical. There was an act of self-fashioning outside of the wanting.

Between twelve and eighteen, I had sex with people my own age, and I had sex in places where they could safely assume I was eighteen, but I could list most of the people I desired. There was the Dorm Master. There was a cluster of boarding-school boys at thirteen. There was the boy at the hospital at fourteen, and a whole cluster of nurses and staff at the hospital I thought of with lust; there was the Farmer when I was sixteen. There were bathhouses and porn theatres when I was seventeen and eighteen. There was the missionary. Those years were a mark of frustration. I refused to think that young people had no sexual thoughts, no desires, no hungers.

There is no room for fondness in this dialogue, no room for autonomy or pleasure. I was a strange child, a child who was not well liked or considered. It was easy to exploit me, and it is easy to think that I made autonomous choices. The list of people I wanted to sleep with is not the same as the people I did sleep with; people said no. I thought I was an adult when I was twelve or fifteen, and I thought I had a right to adult pleasures. As an adult, I have arrived at a difficult, and perhaps improper, balance. I wanted the Dorm Master to fuck (widely defined) me, I thought about it, and I was glad when it happened. The Dorm Master wanted to fuck me and made sure that he succeeded. He should not have acted on that wanting, he should have not made it possible for my desires to be fulfilled. I knew that I wanted to fuck older people when I was younger, and sometimes older people knew about those desires. There is this idea that sexuality is delivered by cherubim via satin pillow the minute you turn eighteen. The homophobes all think that a queer kid or a trans kid is an impossible fiction, or even worse, that they continue to be crafted by trauma. I was always a queer kid who wanted to do queer things with queer adults, and a queer kid who wanted to do queer things with queer kids. Some of the queer adults who took care of me allowed for that possibility, and other queer adults stole that possibility from me.

# Lesson Thirteen:
## Daddies Given Unto You

Catholicism for me was a mélange that was not seen in the suburbs. It was the anarchist priests of the 1970s, arrested for pouring pigs' blood on draft records; it was the sexually decadent bodily pleasure of late-nineteenth-century poets, who used the church as a background for heresy and sodomy; it was the heady, intellectual swerve toward the void that marked the theology of nothingness; it was incense and wine and pretty boys in black cassocks and ignoring that I wasn't ever going to fit into a cassock, that I was never going to be able to serve. So, I decided I was going to be Catholic, did the library research and not the real-people research, did the thesis and not the praxis. I went to the church in town for the Rite of Christian Initiation for Adults. There was a person there who wanted to marry a Catholic, and someone who was working in the Catholic school division and wanted to climb the corporate ladder, and then there was me. Single and queer, connecting more to authority than the rest of them. Youth group with the Mormons on Tuesday; church work with the Catholics on Thursday; gay social group on Friday. It solved where I wanted to land.

I had to be baptized because the Mormons weren't real Christians (something about the one-in-three, three-in-one God of Orthodox Christianity, and the real flesh of God, and the possibility of more than one God in Mormonism – it's messy, it's complex, and it's hidden). There were two events: one at the local church, where I invited my Presbyterian grandmother, who travelled from Calgary to see her queer grandkid denounce Satan and declare loyalty to the pope; one at the cathedral, where my mother bought me a new suit for the occasion.

I was a good Catholic for a few years – a very good Catholic. I went to Catholic conferences, I prayed the rosary, I made a pilgrimage to the Alberta town of Lac St. Ane, whose waters are supposed to heal. I went to youth groups with impossibly handsome young men and deeply pious young women – they had me over for Thanksgiving, for Halloween, for movie nights. I would push against their sexual conservatism, and they would quote Matthew 18:6 to me ('But whoso shall offend one of these little ones which believe in me, it were better for him that a millstone were hanged about his neck, and that he were drowned in the depth of the sea') – and I felt like I was being corrected, their gentleness two thumbs pushed against my throat, which prevented breathing.

I went to the mass where the priests took modern confession. Modern in the sense that I sat in a pew and the priest sat on a chair, and we had a little chat about sin – sin in this slippery, post-humanist way, sin loosely defined as something that separates us from the love of God. Everything separated me from a God whose love I was never convinced of, and the relationality of this made everything float in a haze of good vibes. I wanted the history of severe moral consequences, and I didn't get it.

The booths still existed and the booths were never used. Post–Vatican II confession in a pre–Vatican II church. I would usually go to confession before mass, but a few times, there was a Central European priest who I would wait to talk to. His face looked like it was carved by an axe; he was broad-shouldered, quiet, and intense about my mortal soul. I would confess about sex and he would pretend to speak enough English to understand me. I was flattering myself. The fifth time I talked to him after mass, he spread his hand over his crotch, took my hand and spread it over his hand, nodded, and stood up. He took me through the backrooms of the church, past the vestry, the housekeeping closets, the kitchen, into the domestic spaces – his library, and finally his bedroom. It was 2 p.m. on a Tuesday. There was an iron bed, and above the bed, a large corpus. He led me to the bed and took off his pants.

My pants around my ankles, no underwear, no condom, he messed me up the ass. The corpus was staring down at me, the iron bedstead was rattling against the plaster wall of his bedroom. I gasped and he put his hand over my face, his cock and his hand lacked the tenderness that he had had five minutes before. He was worried I would make noise and I was worried that the cross would fall off the wall. Half-hard, he had both hands on my shoulders – he was shorter than me, the hair on his chest pressed against my back. He lifted his body to fit into mine, thrust quickly and again with efficiency that mercy has evaded. He didn't even give me the honour of reaching around.

The father didn't speak English, and yet we found a mutual language that allowed us to communicate our most basic needs. I confessed the casual lust in my heart, confessing to him about how I masturbated was a turn-on, a sin to confess, which led to another sin to confess, which led to more confessions and more sins, ratcheting up, quarters in the slot machine to an unanticipated jackpot. Being a brat could get me the rewards I had always wanted, the body of Christ being made literal as it shoved Himself into my willing ass, and the body of Christ watching the heresy I was hoping would be sanctified. Father as in priest, Father as in God, Father as Daddy. Foucault called confession a 'continuous incitement to discourse and to truth'; I found out that the right kind of discourse, the right kind of performative truth-telling in the right kind of direction, might get me what I wanted. Even that which was supposed to be private would end up as public (I am writing about confession, which is supposed to be private; and I am writing about the priest fucking me, which is supposed to be private – every secret, if crafted well enough, becomes its own currency, its own token for public entertainments), the movement between the private and the public collapsed, and if you were hungry enough, sometimes you were rewarded. Maybe I was less confused than I thought.

# Lesson Fourteen:
## The Academic Daddy

**M**y friends moved to Toronto and so I moved to Toronto. I left Edmonton because I was burnt out, because I was scared of being stuck in the same place for the rest of my life, and because I was convinced that I had done everything that I could have done there. It was a question of etiquette. I had learned the etiquette of a city and wanted to know if that etiquette scaled.

Balancing the drowning in Toronto's sensory excess and the aridness of Edmonton was unfeasible until my Calgary grandmother died. There was a $20,000 inheritance. Once the money cleared, I immediately went back to Toronto. I pushed every contact I had, dragged every step up the ladder. I used that money well. It got me into the theology school, a WASP bastion inside a WASP bastion. My old boarding school was the country cousin and the feral space, but it was a private Anglican school, connected by coterie – there was a thick line of deliverance. Theology school worked as a finishing school for these boys, and the church would return teachers and administrators. The money worked in a circle, and with my grandmother's old-school manners and her membership in the Imperial Order Daughters of the Empire, the two years of boarding school prayers, the curiosity about old-money rituals, nothing was ever smooth, but with the handshake, which led to a handshake, which led to an entrance, the WASP networks made it work, just a little bit.

The man who was supposed to be my supervisor was kind but quiet and shy. He was a minor Canadian theologian but could have been major – his mind was agile, though he served mostly as a bureaucrat, helping work on a book of saints, helping rewrite the book of services on liturgy and hymns. His classes were too early, and I missed them as much as I attended, but he walked me to the common room after the ones I attended. He answered my emails and was generous and calm. The old kind of Cambridge fellow as a positive model. Another kind of homosociality. He died suddenly in my second year. He never got to supervise my thesis.

My proposed thesis was on the seventeeth-century devotional poet Richard Crashaw. Crashaw was mostly hidden by his contemporaries – too weird and too bodily, not skilled enough to hide his fetishes. He was discovered again in the theory boom of the mid-1990s by the queer theorist Richard Rambuss. Crashaw writes a lot about the body of Christ, but in horrific fashion, about the gaps and holes of the body – ending meaning the absence of flesh, writing on a body that was ragged and rotting. It was miserable work – to impose a queer will, but a queer will without joy. There is this Crashaw poem where he talks about Christ having ten thousand eyes, and each of these eyes wept, but not water, blood.

I wanted to go through a series of poems Crashaw wrote in the seventeenth century and trace these bodily metaphors, these grotesqueries. I think because I found my body grotesque, and my suffering a ready metaphor, because my desire could be made to be sanctified in this kind of bizarre recognition, I wondered if I could make the rent orifices of Christ a minor administrative task, the way I lifted the chalice or distributed the wafers. If my supervisor were queer and not out, and I was queer and performatively out, what would have happened if I'd sat next to that man, shoulder to shoulder, working through a revision of a text? What metaphors would have emerged in that space – unpack, unravel, consume, consider?

There is a joke about Easter: What was the best thing about fucking Jesus after the resurrection? Extra orifices. Crashaw's imagination allowed a thousand orifices, a thousand new ways of inserting meaning in a body that was ripe for insertion. Would studying with the late professor have been another metaphor for failed bodies; would it have been more misery or more joy? We are all apparently part of the body of Christ – there is that Caravaggio painting with Thomas sticking his finger into the body of the risen Lord; there is the passage in the gospels where Thomas slides his whole hand into the side of Christ, wound as womb. The body is a text is a body is a metaphor is a realness returned. Would writing with the professor about the body of Christ via Crashaw have rendered a new body, a new kind of queer resurrection?

I got a master's of theology, and, tired of the insularity, bored, and broke, I decided to search for another kind of pleasure, this one slightly more secular. I went to a school in Montreal to work for an Anglican priest who wrote eloquently and openly about his queer desires – for men, but also for the broken, the askew, the akimbo, and the isolated.

The school was a disaster, but this priest was not.

It was like I had been trained to see 'through the glass darkly,' and then someone said it was no longer necessary. This new priest said in seminars that the adolescent training of other priests, nominally supposed to teach him celibacy, taught him queerness instead, though queerness and celibacy functioned together – one fed the other. Celibates would argue that there was nothing queerer than saying no to that which the culture valued, and radical Catholic queers would argue that strange things grow in the dark; all I thought about was the hinted-at impropriety that was never made clear. Jesuits trained him. What did the Jesuits teach, by inference, by what was real? The explicit boundaries, the tight control of rooms, and the desire sliding out through windows and doors. The instructor went from being Catholic to Anglican, but never lost what he learned from the Jesuits. When he taught us, their ghosts were in the room. The instructor – talking about God and talking about Christ and talking about the men who tried to emulate God and Christ, and talking about sex as power and pleasure – along with everyone around that table, tried very hard to make sure that the Daddy was absent, and like celibacy, the Daddy who was absent became the Daddy who was present.

The Daddy as ghost, the Daddy as monster, the Daddy as post-corporeal, the Daddy as residue, the Daddy as historical figure, the Daddy who was real by not being real. We had a conference session in the professor's name a few years after the class and he skipped it – being talked about and not being present, another kind of Daddy. A Daddy who I talked about sex with but didn't want to sleep with and didn't fantasize about, someone who told me what to do, and who I pushed back on, brattish.

I wanted to make the lessons of the church explicit, and he pushed me away. I wanted to write my final paper on a cluster of sexual assaults that happened in expensive private schools throughout Canada from the 1970s to the mid-1990s, both by students and teachers. James Hill, Leigh Seville, and John Aimers were accused by more than thirty boys of sexual assault at Selwyn House in Montreal. There was a $5 million settlement. Selwyn House, the prestigious boys school in Westmount, had alumni who included captains of industry and prime ministers. Lorne Cook, a teacher at Upper Canada College in Toronto, conducted mock surgeries on his students, as described in the *Globe and Mail*:

> All of the complainants accused him of improprieties when they were in Grade 7. Some of the abuse occurred during the mock transplants, which had students dress up as patients and doctors and involved attaching a catheter resembling a condom joined to a tube to the penis of the 'patient.'

This is not counting the lawsuits and settlements for students attacking other children. There was Robert Farnsworth, the son of headmaster Charles Farnsworth, of Grenville College in Eastern Ontario. He was accused of assaulting children as young as six.

These were just the Anglican schools in Ontario and Quebec. I wanted to write with my supervisor on this subject. I was told that the ethics would be impossible to pass. There were things that I knew would have been difficult to say in public, due to social pressure and lawsuits.

I was broken and exhausted. So, instead, I worked on a biographical analysis of Edmund Wood. This was not unrelated to the work described above. Wood was the founder of St. John's Red Roof and the Lower Canada College. He was considered a kind of house saint among Anglo Anglicans in Montreal. There was a small hagiography written about him by a parish minister, and some of his records were at LCC and at McCord. The hagiography was thin but intriguing. Printed on an inkjet printer, bound in coil from Staples or the equivalent, with some historical photos and some photos from the compiler's trips to England. There were discussions of Wood's younger companion, Albert, a trip they took back to England, Wood's never marrying, his taking care of Albert. There was some discussion of his money – that he didn't make enough for his lifestyle. There was a note or two about the founding of the school – that it moved in the middle of a cold winter, that it was closely attached to the church before it moved. He was an Edwardian figure – and recognizable as one. I wrote around Woods. I wrote about his care of the poor, which seemed self-serving. I wrote about the history of the slums.

Here I was, a queer person doing research for a gay man about a historical queer figure in a church we were all part of. Some of that research, I think, was to say exactly what Albert was doing with Edmund in the back of the church, in the boat back to England, in the carriage to his rich friend's house. He didn't keep letters or diaries. There is a gut feeling or instinct, there is pattern recognition. Wood was swish enough that other queer folks in Montreal recognized him as one of their own, and he was the house saint of the faggiest church in Montreal – even if he never put his mouth or cock anywhere near his younger companion, there was a certain family resemblance. I suspect that he was celibate, or he coded as celibate – but one can still be celibate and deeply, deeply queer.

There is an image of Wood and the boy he lived with stand ing on the deck of a ship, returning for a while to England. In that picture, the lover and the son are collapsed into a single category, and the pedagogical is made explicit. There are other lessons, but sex, desire (despite Freud's dire warning), is not singularly libidinal. At that moment, the ambivalence of the family relationship is made clear.

This priest graded my thesis churlishly. He thought it was sloppy, messy, uncontained, that it didn't prove any of those suppositions. It was too glossy, too gossipy. Again and again, my failure to understand the lessons in question.

# One Last Lesson

The Dorm Master touched my penis, then he disappeared and I attended that school for another year. The tenderness that he expressed was absent, and cruelty replaced it. I would hear about him via whispers, people I knew at the school, like the emergence of a kind of social media. Once, I ran into him at the mall. We had coffee when I was seventeen and I tried to figure out exactly what damage had occurred. At a Tim Horton's downtown, we sat and made small talk, mostly about my religious choices. There was a hotel across the street, and at that moment all I wanted was for him to take me to a room, for me to show him that I had learned my lessons well, that I had become the man that he was training me for. But we didn't.

Instead, when I was forty, a full and complete adult, jettisoning any amount of manhood, I faced him at trial. For almost thirty years, he was an erotic fantasy, a phantasm that went bump in the night, a father figure I was scared of, a Daddy I was turned on by, grown large in the dark, an all-consuming obsession, a therapist's focus, a priest's confessional mode – but none of it flesh.

The Crown attorney would prep me, not well, but he tried. He tried on pronouns, he tried on strategy, and he tried to figure out how to make this queer, scared kid into a presentable adult.

Academics are not supposed to be good witnesses – they are too used to arguing nuance, too sure of their own cleverness, inaccessible. I was all of those things on the stand, but I also wanted the Dorm Master to love me. I felt that if we had a few minutes in a backroom, I could convince the Dorm Master that what we had was real, that he would confess – 'Cowboy take me away' in all the post-Chicks hyper-romanticism. Instead, I stared at him for two days and said to sixteen strangers – and to the man who fucked me at twelve – that I was a chaotic and terrible child, that I was a child unworthy of the love he gave me.

The trial was supposed to make orderly the bodily disorder that was central to my life. Yet the more the defence lawyer talked about sex as an example, against bodies, the more and more abstracted the idea of bodies became – flesh became paperwork, of all things. Most of the questions from the defence lawyer were about the material space. The spanking and the touching occurred at the end of a long hallway. To the left were the Grade 7 dorms, to the right were the Grades 10 and 11 dorms, next door were the classrooms. For the defence, there were too many people, too many witnesses, too much risk, when I was being touched. The defence lawyer furnished building permits, blueprints, and other documents. The paperwork made up for the flesh.

The flesh returns again and again, though. In the pretrial motions, the defence attorney became obsessed with collecting material about my psychiatric history. The Crown attorney asked me to find every hospital admin, therapist, psychiatrist, general practitioner, social worker, and educational assistant that I ever had and to have them gather everything that was ever written about me. The judge shut down the enterprise about halfway through. But there was a subtext here that saw the sum of my experiences and my memories only in terms of records. I was supposed to be made wholly available to the court in files. The court could not imagine me as a body working in conjunction with – and consenting or not consenting to – other bodies, which is how I imagined the narrative.

At times, I would have to imagine flesh where there had been none. The defence lawyer was convinced that we signed in to be spanked, and that there was some kind of double book-keeping system: I signed in, was spanked, he signed the register, and then he brought the register to the headmaster, who signed off on it. None of this happened. There was no register. But I wondered about the paperwork. If he had had to sign off on the spanking, would that have limited what he did? Would it have stopped him from touching my cock? Would that have required its own additional notarization, like good high-church folks for whom no ritual could exist without a written-down liturgy, bound between two covers? Quite literally, the court was papering over my body, but the paper could nonetheless be a sign of the body, and the bodies, underneath.

Still, to this day, I imagine flesh. The Dorm Master taught me how to fuck, to be desired, to be treated as a gentle and dedicated object of devotion; the Dorm Master saw what I wanted, and he gave it to me. The violence in the school – none of that I wanted, none of that was under my control, and I had no say in how the Dorm Master touched my body and usurped my desires. But in the privacy of my own head, in those sweet, quiet moments, I could imagine a life where fucking him was an act of liberation.

I thought about some of this when I left the court, when I got home, when I had to endure the seemingly endless appeals.

I mostly thought about the Crown attorney, though. By 'thought' I mean that I fantasized about him, about how his voice had a drawl, and how he pitched that drawl slow and deep to ingratiate himself. He was trying to make me behave, to make his case, and in his way he was trying to seduce. And then I saw him in the small town for the trial, where we shared a custodian room. The Crown couldn't talk of the trial to me, except in blandnesses, and the voice saying nothing but comforting nonsense was hot, coming from his silly formal suit, inherited from the British, with detachable stiffened cotton cuffs and collar. There was a cop who looked after the chamber and communicated between the judge and the lawyer. Sometimes the cop and the lawyer and I were all in that custodian room together. At night I would masturbate thinking about the cop dropping to his knees, servicing the cock of the lawyer – a cock I could see as a bulge and a hint behind his black trousers.

On the second-to-last day of my testimony, after we discussed sex and real estate in equal measure, the lawyer and I chatted while he took off his jacket, put it away in a garment bag, and undid his cuffs and tie. Nothing was sexier than this stripping formality from his body and speech. Then he realized that he had said what he needed to say, and he left the room, and I saw him going left to the parking lot. I called after him. He didn't turn around. It's as if I was a job, and the job got done, and he never had to say anything again. The lawyer had a wife and kids; he talked about both as small talk before the trial started – he didn't know how to make any other small talk with me. Another Daddy, another loss; that perfect ass in discount leisurewear walking away from me.

I was very obedient, I did everything that was asked of me, I allowed myself to be controlled, and now I wanted, as a reward, to control him a little bit. The mutual control was part of the message, just as I got hard when the Dorm Master pulled me over his knee, just as I imagined the erotic power of the Farmer's quiet sternness; the lawyer could have done anything. I have thought about one fantasy consistently since the trial ended. It is late at night. I am at the Best Western. The night clerk is on a break. I am dealing with email or watching bad television. There is a knock on the door, and I answer it. In my jeans, in a button-up half-open. I don't know who it could be. The lawyer is at the door. He's wearing worn-out khakis and a stretched-out polo. He invites himself into the room, strides across it, shuts the curtains, turns off the TV, sweeps my stuff off the desk. Sitting down in a chair, he tells me to sit on the bed. He takes out my paperwork, he goes over arguments, he stretches, and bends, and shoves his body into my space, at first symbolically, then literally. He goes to the washroom; hearing him piss, I get half-hard. He walks out with his belt buckle undone, his zipper down. He puts his hand over my mouth, his mouth over my cock, I lick his hand like a dog slobbering over a good piece of rawhide.

Last month, I had a new friend, a carpenter, with slippery politics, though pious and handsome in equal measure. He was half shit-talking a friend of his, and he used the word *scamp*. Nothing was more erotic in recent memory than someone calling someone else scamp – sort of a rascal, that good-boy/bad-boy kind of energy. I wanted him to scratch behind my ears, to call me scamp, to call me a good boy.

Fucking the Crown attorney is the ultimate good-boy energy, scamp makes sense, good scamp energy – because I am not a boy, and not a girl, just a host for someone better than me to tell me that I did a good job, and in that guttural Calvinist mode.

As a reward, I imagine the Crown attorney finishes all over those legal documents, sealing them in a way the court doesn't recognize.

Even imagining myself as a sub in a cheap hotel room in the middle of the prairie gives me more practical autonomy than actually being a witness under the same circumstances. The Dorm Master was convicted; it was in the public record what he did. He appealed and I left, unsatisfied. The dissatisfaction and our mutual refusing to accept what we both know is itself a lesson. But when you are an adult, you understand the gulf between wanting and getting. Reject gender, reject authority, reject the body, reject God, reject the dualism of goodness and badness, reject the idea that hard work will get you into heaven, and yet all I want is to be on my knees, with a cock in my mouth, eyes staring up, and have someone tell me that I am doing a good job, that I am a good person. All I want is to talk until I am forced to shut up. All I want is for my body to reassert itself, not when it is hungry or sore, but in pleasure. I want to fall apart with grace and elegance, I want to get up off my knees, wipe my lips, another completed task; but Daddy won't let me.

And maybe I don't really want it.

I know that Daddy isn't good for me, and I want a Daddy anyway.

## Books

Allison, Dorothy. *Trash: Short Stories*. Michigan: Firebrand Books, 1988.

Barthes, Roland. *A Lover's Discourse: Fragments*. Translated by Richard Howard. New York: Farrar, Straus and Giroux, 1978.

Boccaccio, Giovanni. *The Decameron*. Translated by G. H. McWilliam. London: Penguin Classics, 2003.

Burgess, Preston. *Confessions of a Married Man*. New York: Lancer Books, 1966.

Califia, Patrick. *Macho Sluts: A Little Sister's Classic*. Vancouver: Arsenal Pulp Press, 2009.

Delany, Samuel R. *Hogg*. Utah: Black Ice Books, 2003.

———. *The Motion of Light on Water*. New York: Arbor House, 1988.

———. *Times Square Red, Times Square Blue*. New York: New York University Press, 1999.

Foucault, Michel. *The History of Sexuality: An Introduction*. New York: Vintage Books, 1990.

Greenwell, Garth. *Cleanness*. New York: Farrar, Straus and Giroux, 2020.

Guibert, Hervé. *To the Friend Who Did Not Save My Life*. Los Angeles: Semiotext(e), 2020.

Hocquenghem, Guy, and René Schérer. *Co-Ire*. Translated by Irene Windsor. https://homintern.soy/issues/11-9-20/comingandgoingtogether.html.

James, Lorelei. *Corralled*. New York: Berkley, 2013.

———. *One Night Rodeo*. New York: Signet, 2016.

———. *Saddled and Spurred*. New York: Signet, 2011.

———. *Wrangled and Tangled*. New York: Signet Eclipse, 2011.

Koestenbaum, Wayne. 'Darling's Prick.' *The Next American Essay*. Edited by John D'Agata. Minneapolis: Greywolf Press, 2003.

Réage, Pauline. *The Story of O*. Paris: Olympia Press, 1965.

Rambuss, Richard. *Closet Devotions*. North Carolina: Duke University Press, 1998.

Sade, Marquis de. *Justine, or The Misfortunes of Virtue*. Translated by John Phillips. Oxford: Oxford University Press, 2013.

———. *The 120 Days of Sodom*. Translated by Will McMorran and Thomas Wynn. London: Penguin Classics, 2016.

Salter, James. *A Sport and a Pastime*. New York: Doubleday, 1967.

Sedgwick, Eve Kosofsky. *Epistemology of the Closet*. Los Angeles: University of California Press, 2008.

Sturgis, Matthew. *Oscar Wilde: A Life*. New York: Knopf, 2021.

## News

Appleby, Timothy. 'Retired UCC Teacher Guilty in Sex Case,' *Globe and Mail*, October 13, 2006. https://www.theglobe andmail.com/news/national/retired-ucc-teacher-guilty-in-sex-case/article4111899.

Fowlie, Jonathan. 'Ex-Teacher Faces Charge of Abuse,' *Globe and Mail*, April 8, 2004. https://www.theglobeandmail.com/news/national/ex-teacher-faces-charge-of-abuse/article18281004.

Sawa, Timothy, Andrew Culbert, and Bob McKeown. 'New Sex Abuse Allegations Target Son of Former Headmaster at Now-Closed Christian Boarding School,' *CBC News*, January 20, 2022. https://www.cbc.ca/news/canada/new-allegations-school-of-secrets-1.6319539.

'Selwyn House Ignored Sex-Abuse Claim for 20 Years: Documents,' *CBC News*, August 7, 2008, https://www.cbc.ca/news/canada/montreal/selwyn-house-ignored-sex-abuse-claim-for-20-years-documents-1.709947.

## Poems

Crashaw, Richard. *Steps to the Temple: Sacred Poems, with Other Delights of the Muses*. London: Humphrey Moseley, 1646; Ann Arbor: Text Creation Partnership, 2011, p. 22, http://name.umdl.umich.edu/A34930.0001.001.

Housman, A. E. *A Shropshire Lad and Other Poems*. London: Penguin Classics, 2010.

O'Hara, Frank. 'Ava Maria.' In *Lunch Poems*. San Francisco: City Lights Books, 1964.

Whitman, Walt. *Leaves of Grass: A Norton Critical Edition*. Deathbed edition, edited by Sculley Bradley and Harold W. Blodgett, section XI. New York: W. W. Norton & Company, 1973.

## Essays

Fox, Charlie. 'Crazy for Vincent,' *Frieze*, March 16, 2017, https://www.frieze.com/article/crazy-vincent.

Hickey, Dave. 'Glass Bottom Cadillac.' In *Air Guitar: Essays on Art & Democracy*. Los Angeles: Art Issues Press, 1997.

Sedgwick, Eve Kosofsky. 'A Poem Is Being Written.' *Representations*, no. 17 (Winter 1987): 110–43. https://doi.org/10.2307/3043795.

Stone, Sandy. 'The *Empire* Strikes Back: A Posttranssexual Manifesto.' *Transgender Studies Reader*. London: Routledge, 2006.

## Tracts/Scripture/Religious Work

The Anglican Church of Canada. *The Book of Common Prayer*. Toronto: Anglican Book Centre, 1962.

The Church of Jesus Christ of Latter-day Saints. *For the Strength of Youth*. Utah: The Church of Jesus Christ of Latter-day Saints, 1990. https://issuu.com/vintageldspamphlets/docs/for-the-strength-of-youth-1990.

———. *For the Strength of Youth: A Guide for Making Choices*. Utah: The Church of Jesus Christ of Latter-day Saints, 2022. https://www.churchofjesuschrist.org/study/manual/for-the-strength-of-youth?lang=eng.

Hinckley, Gordon B. 'The First Presidency and Council of the Twelve Apostles of the Church of Jesus Christ of Latter-day Saints.' Proclamation read at the General Relief Society Meeting, Salt Lake City, Utah, September 1995. https://www.churchofjesuschrist.org/bc/content/shared/content/english/pdf/36035_000_24_family.pdf.

Luke 12:2–3.

Matthew 18:6.

Packer, Boyd K. 'To Young Men Only.' Address given at the Priesthood Session of General Conference, Salt Lake City, Utah, October 1976. https://archive.org/stream/ToYoung-MenOnly/To%20Young%20Men%20Only_djvu.txt.

## Songs/Albums

Amos, Tori. *Boys for Pele*. Atlantic Records, 1996, CD.

Beyoncé. 'Church Girl.' Track 7 on *Renaissance*. Columbia Records, 2022, CD.

Boney M. 'Rasputin.' Track 2 on *Nightlight to Venus*. Atlantic, 1978, CD.

Brooks, Garth. 'Friends in Low Places.' Track 5 on *No Fences*. Capitol Nashville, 1990, CD.

Brooks and Dunn. 'Boot Scootin' Boogie.' Track 8 on *Brand New Man*. Arista, 1991, CD.

Byrd, Tracy. 'Watermelon Crawl.' Track 5 on *No Ordinary Man*. MCA, 1994, CD.

Harvey, PJ. 'Sheela-Na-Gig.' Track 6 on *Dry*. Too Pure, 1992, CD.

———. '50ft Queenie.' Track 8 on *Rid of Me*. Island, 1993, CD.

Hole. 'Doll Parts.' Track 6 on *Live Through This*. DGC, 1994, CD.

Jennings, Waylon. 'Are You Sure Hank Done It This Way.' Track 1 on *Dreaming My Dream*. RCA Victor, 1975, CD.

Led Zeppelin. 'Stairway to Heaven.' Track 4 on *Led Zeppelin IV*. Atlantic, 1971, CD.

Moore, Kip. 'Somethin' 'Bout a Truck.' Track 3 on *Up All Night*. MCA Nashville, 2012, CD.

Nitty Gritty Dirt Band. 'Cadillac Ranch.' Track 8 on *Plain Dirt Fashion*. Warner Bros Nashville, 1984, CD.

Savage Garden. 'Truly Madly Deeply.' Track 5 on *Savage Garden*. Columbia Records, 1997, CD.

Sixpence None the Richer. 'Kiss Me.' Track 4 on *Sixpence None the Richer*. Squint, 1997, CD.

Stealers Wheel. 'Stuck in the Middle with You.' Track 2 on *Stealers Wheel*. A&M, 1972, CD.

Taylor, Frances K. 'Daddy's Homecoming.' 1989. https://www.churchofjesuschrist.org/music/library/childrens-songbook/daddys-homecoming?lang=eng.

Twitty, Conway, and Loretta Lynn. 'As Soon as I Hang Up the Phone.' Track 1 on *Country Partners*. MCA, 1974, CD.

Watkins, Vanja Y., and Ruth Muir Gardner. 'Families Can Be Together Forever.' 1980. https://www.churchofjesuschrist.org/music/library/childrens-songbook/families-can-be-together-forever?lang=eng.

## Films

Jordan, Neil, dir. *The End of the Affair*. 1999; Culver City, CA: Sony Pictures Releasing, 2000, DVD.

LaBute, Neil, dir. *Your Friends & Neighbors*. 1998; Universal City, CA: Gramercy Pictures, 1999, DVD.

Poole, Wakefield, dir. *Boys in the Sand*. 1971; New York: Poole-mar, DVD.

Reichenbach, François, dir. *Nus masculins*. 1954; France.

Schlesinger, John, dir. *Midnight Cowboy*. 1969; New York: Criterion Collection, Blue Ray.

Sharman, Jim, dir. *The Rocky Horror Picture Show*. 1975; Los Angeles: Twentieth Century Fox, 2000, DVD.

Tarantino, Quentin, dir. *Reservoir Dogs*. 1994; Los Angeles: Miramax Films, 1997, DVD.

## Performances

Rolling Rockvideos. 'PJ Harvey at Glastonbury Festival 24 Jun 1995 Full Show.' YouTube. May 10, 2020. Video, 59:25. https://www.youtube.com/watch?v=Fbrtd4ezE3Y.

## Plays

LaBute, Neil. *bash: latterday plays*. New York: Harry N. Abrams, Inc., 1999.

## Locations *(in order of appearance)*

Edmonton Alberta Bonnie Doon Stake Centre
Cardston Alberta Temple
Basement of Fort Saskatchewan Public Library

North Saskatchewan River near Devon
Anon Bar on Bourbon Street in New Orleans
440 Castro in San Francisco
Fox Cinema
Continental Baths Edmonton
Times Square Books & Magazine in downtown Edmonton
Times Square Books, Stony Plain Road, Edmonton
Ponoka Rodeo Ground
Ponoka Stampeder Inn
Coliseum Inn in Edmonton – permanently closed
Greyhound Station in Red Deer – permanently closed
Adolescent Psych Ward, Edmonton
Concordia University's Department of Religions and Cultures
Trinity College, University of Toronto
Wycliffe College, University of Toronto

## Other

Ryman, Robert. *Untitled*. 1976. Pastel and graphite on plexiglass
    with square black oxide steel fasteners and hex bolts, 126.1
    × 126.1 cm. Museum of Modern Art.
Michelangelo. *Dying Slave*. 1513–16. Marble, 229 cm. Louvre
    Museum.
Kiwanga, Kapwani. *A wall is just a wall (and nothing more at
    all)*. February 3–May 6, 2018. Art exhibition. Calgary: Esker
    Foundation, 2018.
Canadian National Exhibition mini-donuts
Serge Lutens La Fille de Berlin (fragrance)
Pilsner, or Pil (beer)
Peter Jackson (cigarettes)

# Acknowledgements

For Ben and Carl, who are my best, first readers.

For Erika and Andrea, two careful readers whose rigorous notes made me less anxious.

For Patrick, for two decades of close friendship.

For Martin, in queer solidarity.

For Kristy, whose radical empathy I try to emulate every day.

For D – I remember every waiting room and courthouse, every ward, and most clinics.

For Ray, who keeps saying that I cannot make a career out of wanting to fuck straight boys; I hope this disproves him.

For Travis, for the germaniums, the irises, the lilacs, the ongoing conversations about paintings, and the continual notice that beauty is political.

For David, in autistic solidarity.

For Glenys, who heard these stories for decades before they ended on paper.

And for JM, for enduring two years of listening about this book.

**Steacy Easto**n is a writer and visual artist originally from Edmonton, who has lived in Hamilton for more than seven years. They have written on gender, sexuality, and country music for publications including *Slate*, NPR, and the *Atlantic Online*. Upcoming books include *Why Tammy Wynette Matters* for University of Texas and a 33⅓ volume for Bloomsbury. They were the 2022 Martha Street Studio resident artist in Winnipeg.

Typeset in Arno and Romana.

Printed at the Coach House on bpNichol Lane in Toronto, Ontario, on Zephyr Antique Laid paper, which was manufactured, acid-free, in Saint-Jérôme, Quebec, from second-growth forests. This book was printed with vegetable-based ink on a 1973 Heidelberg KORD offset litho press. Its pages were folded on a Baumfolder, gathered by hand, bound on a Sulby Auto-Minabinda, and trimmed on a Polar single-knife cutter.

Coach House is on the traditional territory of many nations, including the Mississaugas of the Credit, the Anishnabeg, the Chippewa, the Haudenosaunee, and the Wendat peoples, and is now home to many diverse First Nations, Inuit, and Métis peoples. We acknowledge that Toronto is covered by Treaty 13 with the Mississaugas of the Credit. We are grateful to live and work on this land.

Edited by Tamara Faith Berger, seen through the press by Crystal Sikma
Cover design by Crystal Sikma
Interior design by Crystal Sikma
Author photo by Jesse Driftwood

Coach House Books
80 bpNichol Lane
Toronto ON M5S 3J4
Canada

mail@chbooks.com
www.chbooks.com